THE LIFE OF

FRANK HYLAND
FOREWORD BY PRISCILLA PRESLEY

Whitman
Publishing, LLC
PUBLISHING SINCE 1934
www.whitman.com

The Life of Elvis

www.whitman.com

© 2014 Whitman Publishing, LLC.
3101 Clairmont Road, Suite G, Atlanta GA 30329
All photographs copyrighted by Elvis Presley Enterprises, Inc. unless otherwise noted.

Correspondence concerning this book may be directed to the publisher at the address above, attn: The Life of Elvis.

ISBN: 0794842283
Authored in the United States of America
Printed in China

For a catalog of collectibles-related books, supplies and storage products, visit Whitman Publishing online at **www.whitman.com**.

CONTENTS

A LIFETIME OF MEMORIES IN THIS BOOK

From the outside looking in, Elvis was a man who entertained the world, but to me, he was my rock, my best friend, my mentor, my confidant and loving father to our daughter. He has given me a lifetime of memories that I will cherish forever.

On stage, Elvis was a star, but at Graceland, he was a private man who led a very private life, away from the Hollywood limelight. Life at Graceland could be unpredictable. You never knew what Elvis' whim might be, and I learned very quickly to adapt. It was definitely his palace and place of retreat. Today, Graceland still feels like home to me and my daughter, with all of its furnishings, horses roaming the pastures and curious fans at the gate. Fans from all corners of the globe who tour the home step through the same front door as Elvis did, and experience what it is about Graceland that made him feel so safe and secure.

Elvis' story truly is one of rags-to-riches fame. A humble beginning in Tupelo would keep him close to his roots, even when he was on top of the world. With sold-out shows and major record deals, he remembered where he came from by keeping his family and friends close at hand. His talent and good looks along with his humility and kind nature endeared him not only to me, but millions of adoring fans.

I am reminded of just how sentimental Elvis was when I am in Memphis and I see some of the things he saved that we now keep in our guarded Graceland Archives.

One of my favorite artifacts is a set of bongo drums that I gave him during our first Christmas together in Germany. I asked my father for money to buy him a gift. I remember walking on the streets of Wiesbaden,

Priscilla holds a photo of Elvis in Wiesbaden, Germany, where the two met in 1959. The two began dating and while the world knew Elvis for his music and movies, Priscilla knew a sweet, sentimental man whom she would eventually marry.

(Above) Elvis looks every bit the proud papa as Priscilla cradles Lisa Marie just days after the couple's daughter was born. (Opposite page) Elvis was sentimental about many of the things he acquired but none more so than the set of bongo drums Priscilla gave him on their first Christmas together in Germany.

endlessly searching for something that would be unique, memorable and special, and constantly asking myself, "what do I buy someone who seemingly has everything?" When I saw them in the store window, I was hoping it was something Elvis didn't already own. I asked, "would he think it's stupid?" and "did he already have them?" — a hundred doubts were going through my mind. At home, I carefully wrapped his gift as if it were a precious stone, proud that I discovered it myself, but still wondering, "would he like them?"

When it was time for us to exchange gifts, Elvis slowly opened his, and his face lit up. It brings a smile to my face knowing he was trying to make me feel good when he commented to one of his friends "bongos, just what I always wanted." Now, those drums — weathered from use and age — are sometimes displayed during Christmas at Graceland, but to me, that old set of bongo drums is a symbol of the sentimental side of Elvis. The fact is, he kept that first gift along with many other things, such as records,

contracts, photos, airline tickets and even letters I wrote to him while I was in Germany and after. Sentimental? Yes, that he could be. That is the Elvis I knew.

The author of this book has gone to great detail to ensure accuracy. Furthering its authenticity is the cooperation of Elvis Presley Enterprises, Inc. and the Graceland staff.

I hope this book leaves you with great memories of Elvis, just as it has revived memories of my own, and that you enjoy it as much as I do.

— Priscilla Presley

DON'T WORRY NONE, BABY

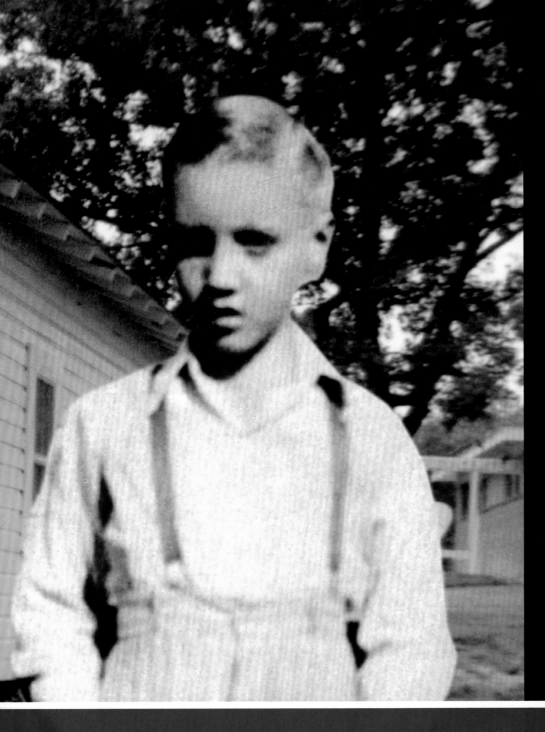

On Oct. 3, 1945, some of the people at the Mississippi-Alabama Fair and Dairy show in Tupelo, Mississippi, saw history in the making. At the urging of his mother and one of his teachers, a 10-year-old boy entered a talent contest, climbed atop a chair to reach a microphone and sang Red Foley's classic, "Old Shep." For his efforts the youngster won fifth-place — $5 worth of fair rides. But it was more than that. It was the first public performance of the Crown Prince of Rock 'n' Roll, the boy who one day would be King, Elvis Presley. Years later, Elvis would remember the event fondly, but also with a bit of melancholy. "They entered me in a talent contest," he said in a 1972 interview, "I wore glasses, had no music and I won. I think it was fifth place. ... I [also] got a whipping the same day, my mother whipped me for something. ... It destroyed my ego completely."

(Preceding page) Elvis Presley's father, Vernon, built this two-room shotgun shack shortly before Elvis' birth, borrowing $180 from dairy farmer Orville Bean to purchase the materials. (Left) Elvis Aron Presley was born on January 8, 1935, along with his twin brother Jessie Garon, who was stillborn.

"When I grow up, I'm going to buy you a house and pay everything you owe at the grocery store and get two Cadillacs."
— Elvis as a youngster to his parents, Gladys and Vernon

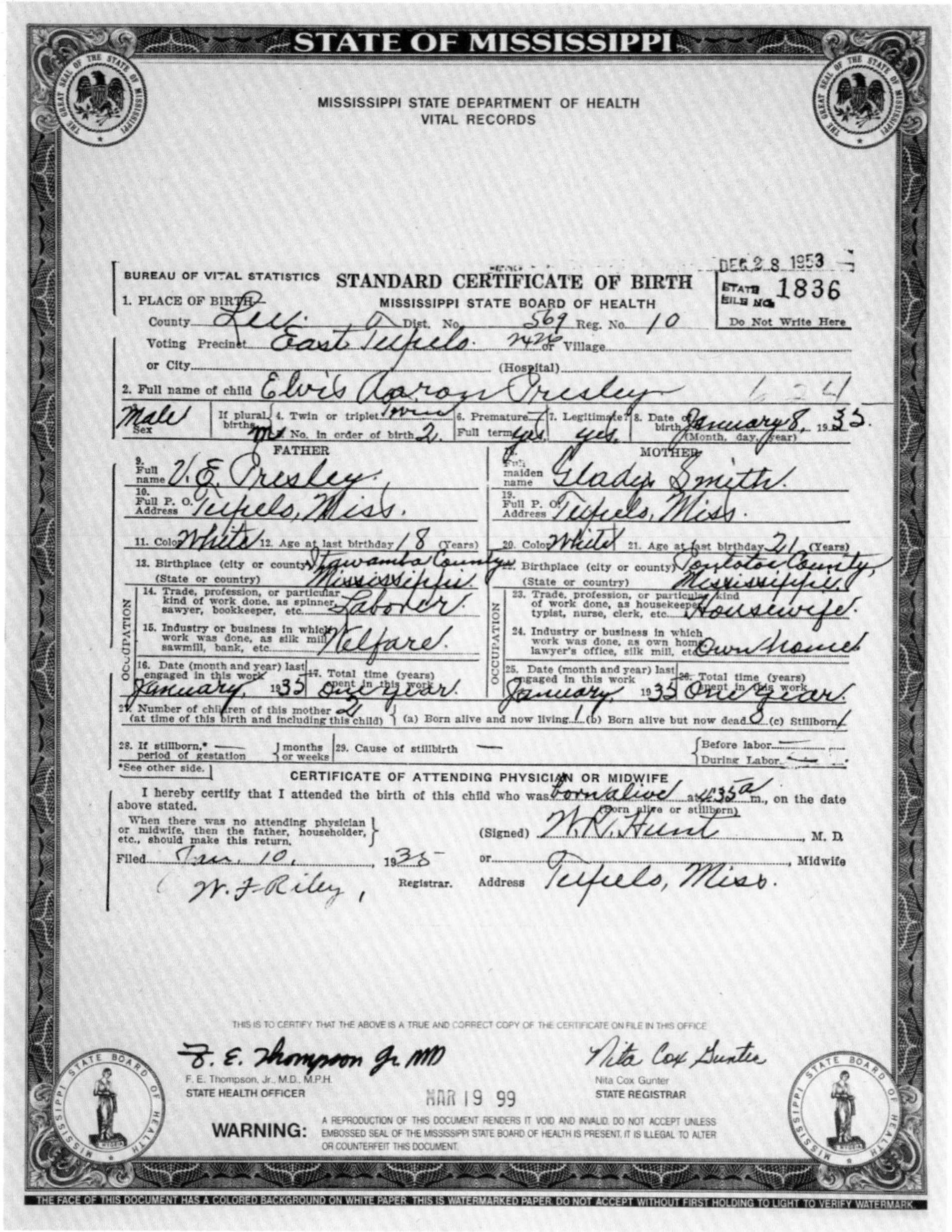

STATE OF MISSISSIPPI

MISSISSIPPI STATE DEPARTMENT OF HEALTH
VITAL RECORDS

BUREAU OF VITAL STATISTICS STANDARD CERTIFICATE OF BIRTH
MISSISSIPPI STATE BOARD OF HEALTH

DEC 28 1953
STATE FILE NO. 1836
Do Not Write Here

1. PLACE OF BIRTH
County Lee Dist. No. 569 Reg. No. 10
Voting Precinct East Tupelo or Village
or City (Hospital)
2. Full name of child Elvis Aaron Presley
3. Sex Male | If plural births: 4. Twin or triplet twin; 5. No. in order of birth 2 | 6. Premature / Full term yes | 7. Legitimate? yes | 8. Date of birth January 8, 1935 (Month, day, year)

FATHER
9. Full name V. E. Presley
10. Full P. O. Address Tupelo, Miss.
11. Color White 12. Age at last birthday 18 (Years)
13. Birthplace (city or county) Itawamba County (State or country) Mississippi
14. Trade, profession, or particular kind of work done, as spinner, sawyer, bookkeeper, etc. Laborer
15. Industry or business in which work was done, as silk mill, sawmill, bank, etc. Welfare
16. Date (month and year) last engaged in this work January, 1935 17. Total time (years) spent in this work One year

MOTHER
18. Full maiden name Gladys Smith
19. Full P. O. Address Tupelo, Miss.
20. Color White 21. Age at last birthday 21 (Years)
22. Birthplace (city or county) Pontotoc County (State or country) Mississippi
23. Trade, profession, or particular kind of work done, as housekeeper, typist, nurse, clerk, etc. Housewife
24. Industry or business in which work was done, as own home, lawyer's office, silk mill, etc. Own home
25. Date (month and year) last engaged in this work January, 1935 26. Total time (years) spent in this work One year

27. Number of children of this mother (at time of this birth and including this child) 2 (a) Born alive and now living 1 (b) Born alive but now dead 0 (c) Stillborn 1
28. If stillborn,* period of gestation — months or weeks 29. Cause of stillbirth — Before labor — During Labor —
*See other side.

CERTIFICATE OF ATTENDING PHYSICIAN OR MIDWIFE
I hereby certify that I attended the birth of this child who was born alive at 4:35 a.m., on the date above stated.
(Born alive or stillborn)
When there was no attending physician or midwife, then the father, householder, etc., should make this return.
(Signed) W. R. Hunt, M. D.
or ...., Midwife
Filed Jan. 10, 1935
W. F. Riley, Registrar. Address Tupelo, Miss.

THIS IS TO CERTIFY THAT THE ABOVE IS A TRUE AND CORRECT COPY OF THE CERTIFICATE ON FILE IN THIS OFFICE

F. E. Thompson Jr. MD
F. E. Thompson, Jr., M.D., M.P.H.
STATE HEALTH OFFICER

MAR 19 99

Nita Cox Gunter
Nita Cox Gunter
STATE REGISTRAR

WARNING: A REPRODUCTION OF THIS DOCUMENT RENDERS IT VOID AND INVALID. DO NOT ACCEPT UNLESS EMBOSSED SEAL OF THE MISSISSIPPI STATE BOARD OF HEALTH IS PRESENT. IT IS ILLEGAL TO ALTER OR COUNTERFEIT THIS DOCUMENT.

THE FACE OF THIS DOCUMENT HAS A COLORED BACKGROUND ON WHITE PAPER. THIS IS WATERMARKED PAPER. DO NOT ACCEPT WITHOUT FIRST HOLDING TO LIGHT TO VERIFY WATERMARK.

TOUGH TIMES IN TUPELO

Elvis probably didn't get whipped too often by his mother, Gladys. He was an only child — his twin brother Jessie Garon had been stillborn — and the apple of his mother's eye. That loving feeling was mutual.

"Don't worry none, Baby," young Elvis often told his mother. "When I grow up, I'm going to buy you a fine house and pay everything you owe at the grocery store and get two Cadillacs, one for you and Daddy and one for me."

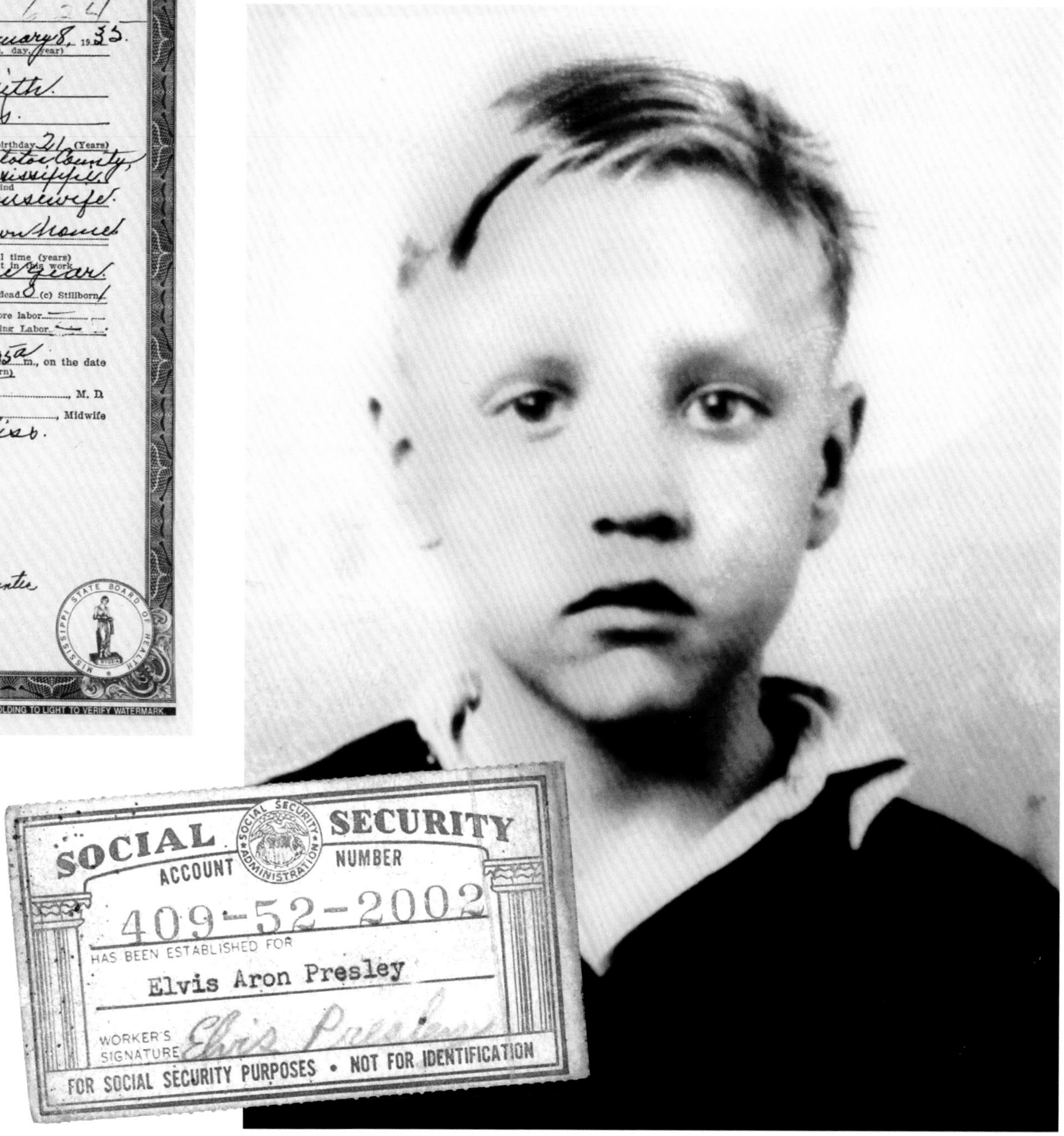

(Preceding page) Vernon and Gladys met at a First Assembly of God Church meeting in East Tupelo and married in Mississippi in 1933, borrowing $3 from friends for the marriage license. (Above) Elvis' middle name appears as "Aaron" on his birth certificate but as "Aron" on his Social Security card and high school diploma. Elvis mostly used "Aron," but later tried to legally change it to "Aaron," whereupon he found out that, to the government at least, he had been Elvis Aaron all along.

That was some pretty big dreaming for a kid who grew up as Elvis did. To say the Presley family was poor would be to say the Rockefellers were modestly rich. Elvis' father, Vernon, worked as a sharecropper and truck driver and, some alleged, ran a bit of whiskey on the side. His mother worked as a sewing machine operator. Times were tough in East Tupelo in those days, and they got tougher when Vernon was sent to prison along with two of his friends for altering a $4 check. The sentence was for three years, but he served only eight months.

Still, that was enough to cost the Presleys the shotgun house Vernon had built, and they spent the next few years banging around Mississippi as Vernon looked for any work he could find. By 1948, the family moved to Memphis and eventually wound up living in a housing project, Lauderdale Courts. Elvis enrolled in L.C. Humes High School, where he studied without any great distinction, but also with no major gaffes, until he graduated in 1953.

(Left) Numerous accounts of Elvis' early life mention the close bond he shared with his mother and her protective nature toward her only son. (Below) Vernon cared deeply for his wife and child, sending Gladys numerous postcards from Parchman Farm, where he was sentenced to serve three years for forging a check when Elvis was just 5.

In 1948 the Presleys moved to Memphis and were soon living in Lauderdale Courts, a collection of public-assistance apartments near downtown.

PHILLIPS, JAMES ARNETT
Major: Science, Special Studies, Drafting, English.
Activities: The Pan, National Forensic, Debate Team, Spanish Club, Hi-Y, Biology Club, History Club, Speech Club, Student Council Representative, Non-Com Officer in R.O.T.C., Vice-President Speech Club, Vice-President History Club.
Awards: Winner District Debate Tournament, Winner "I Speak For Democracy" Contest.

ROBINSON, KATIE MAE
Major: Commercial, Home Ec., English.
Activities: F.H.A., History Club, English Club, Vice-President History Club.

RULEMAN, SHIRLEY
Major: Home Ec., Commercial, English.
Activities: National Honor Society, F.H.A., Y-Teens, Latin Club, Jr. Cheerleader, Sabre Club, History Club, English Club, Honorary Captain in R.O.T.C., President Home Ec. Class.

PRESLEY, ELVIS ARON
Major: Shop, History, English.
Activities: R.O.T.C., Biology Club, English Club, History Club, Speech Club.

PERRY, ROBERT EARL
Major: History, Science, English.
Activities: Biology Club, T&I Club, Key Club, Baseball 4 years, Vice-President Key Club, Boys' Vice-President Senior Class, President T&I Club.
Awards: All-Star American Legion Baseball Team 1952, National Honor Society.

SANDERS, MARY LOUISE
Major: Commercial, Band, English.
Activities: Senior Band, Y-Teens, English Club, History Club, Historian of Band.

SEALY, CAROLYN NAOMI
Major: Commercial, Art, English.
Activities: Fifty Club, Y-Teens, Red Cross, Monitor, Sight-Saving Room.
Award: Merit Award in Lion Oil Essay Contest, Scholastic Golden Key Award in Art.

ROTENBERRY, JAMES RUSSELL
Major: Drafting, Shop, English.
Activities: History Club, English Club, Biology Club, Hi-Y Science Club, President Science Club, Vice-President Biology Club.

ROBINSON, EDWARD McMILLAN

And, all the while he trudged through school and a couple of part-time jobs, he always had his guitar. He had received his first guitar on his 11th birthday — when he really wanted a bicycle — and had been taught to play by his uncle, Vester, his father's brother and his pastor Frank Smith. Despite the early lessons, he wasn't really an accomplished musician. "I don't read music," he later confessed, "but I know what I like."

In 1948, Elvis started coursework at Humes High School (below) where he made a few friends (above) and participated in the Biology Club, the English Club, the History Club, the Speech Club and the ROTC (right).

It wasn't long, either, before Elvis started to sport his trademark sideburns. Though he was basically a shy, reserved kid, the new look made him stand out among his peers.

(Above) By 1953 Elvis had started to sport the style thousands would soon come to know, the swept-up hair and a hint of the famous lip curl. (Right) Elvis and his cousin Gene Smith get their picture taken in Western garb at the 1953 Mid South Fair.

Radio DJ Dewey Phillips often advertised the Lansky Brothers clothing shop on Beale Street, and Elvis, even before he could afford the flashy clothes, was drawn to their bold designs. He window shopped often enough that both Guy and Bernard Lansky knew him by sight.

"I DON'T SOUND LIKE NOBODY"

After graduation, Elvis first went to work for Precision Tool Company before he got a job driving a truck at Crown Electric Company. He began to wear his hair long, swept back in a ducktail, a popular style at the time. Many teens adopted this "greaser" look to go along with black leather jackets and motorcycle boots popularized by another young star, Marlon Brando, in the movie "The Wild One." Only Elvis didn't go for the leather; he preferred flashy outfits — often in pink and black — that he bought at Lansky Brothers on Beale Street once he could afford to.

But above and beyond everything else — the poverty, school, work, everything — the one thing that drove young Elvis was his music, always the music.

One of Elvis' first jobs out of high school was driving a truck, like the one below, for Crown Electric, ferrying materials out to construction sites. He earned $1 per hour and took home $40 a week, unless he worked a bit of overtime at $1.50 per hour.

It had been that way in Tupelo, where he sang in the Assembly of God Church his family attended and later when he sang occasionally (as did a lot of other youngsters in the town) on the amateur hour show on WELO hosted by local legend Mississippi Slim. And once he got that guitar at age 11, Elvis almost always had it with him.

It accelerated in Memphis, then and now a hotbed of music: gospel, blues, hillbilly, jazz, just about anything. For the white audience in the early '50s, the radio voice of music was Dewey Phillips on WHBQ. For the black audience — and a lot of whites also tuned in — there was WDIA, which featured among other performers the legendary B.B. King. At Lauderdale Courts, Elvis and four of his buddies formed what today would be called a garage band. They practiced in the laundry room and sometimes played for the residents in the courtyard on summer nights. In high school, Elvis won a talent contest by playing in front of the entire student body.

(Left) Elvis poses with the Presleys' Lincoln in the early 1950s, a few short years before Cadillacs would become the family staple. (Below) Elvis and a trio of high school friends, Buzzy Forbess (left), Farley Guy and Paul Dougher (not pictured), all lived in the Courts and threw numerous parties at which Elvis most always sang. (Opposite page) It wouldn't be long before Elvis would wander into Sun Studios on Union Avenue, a shy kid looking to record a song as a gift for his mother.

In midsummer 1953, Elvis went to Sun Records to record two songs for $8.25 as a present for his mother. Sun was owned by another who would become a legend in the music industry, Sam Phillips. Elvis didn't see Phillips that day, but did see his assistant, Marion Keisker, who was also a local radio personality. According to Ernst Jorgensen in *Elvis Presley: A Life in Music — The Complete Recording Sessions*, the meeting went something like this:

"What kind of singer are you?" Keisker asked.

"I sing all kinds," Elvis replied.

"Who do you sound like?"

"I don't sound like nobody."

Keisker made a note to herself: "Good ballad singer. Hold."

It held for a year. In the summer of 1954, Sam Phillips was listening to some cuts by Red Wortham called "Without You."

(Right) Elvis paid $8.95 to record "My Happiness," a 1948 Jon and Sandra Steele song, and the Ink Spots'"That's When Your Heartaches Begin." Sun owner Sam Phillips told Elvis he was an "interesting" singer and that he might call him sometime. (Opposite page) Phillips did call Elvis and while Vernon and Gladys were cautiously supportive of their son's fledgling music career, Gladys was happy to see him start attending church again and hoping for him to find a girl to settle down with.

He thought he wanted to record the song with a quavering voice. Keisker suggested Elvis, and Phillips told her to give the kid a call. She did, and according to Elvis later, "I was there before she hung up the phone."

He went into the studio and sang song after song, just about everything he knew. Phillips didn't record any of it, thinking it to be pretty amateurish, but there was still that nagging thought in his mind that this kid had that something he had been looking for. The songs just weren't the right fit, for whatever the reason.

"I was an overnight sensation," Elvis would often tell interviewers later. "After a year, they called me back."

(Below) Phillips continued to work with Elvis in early 1954, trying to find a song that fit the singer's unique voice. (Opposite page) About the same time, Elvis began dating Dixie Locke, a girl he had met at church.

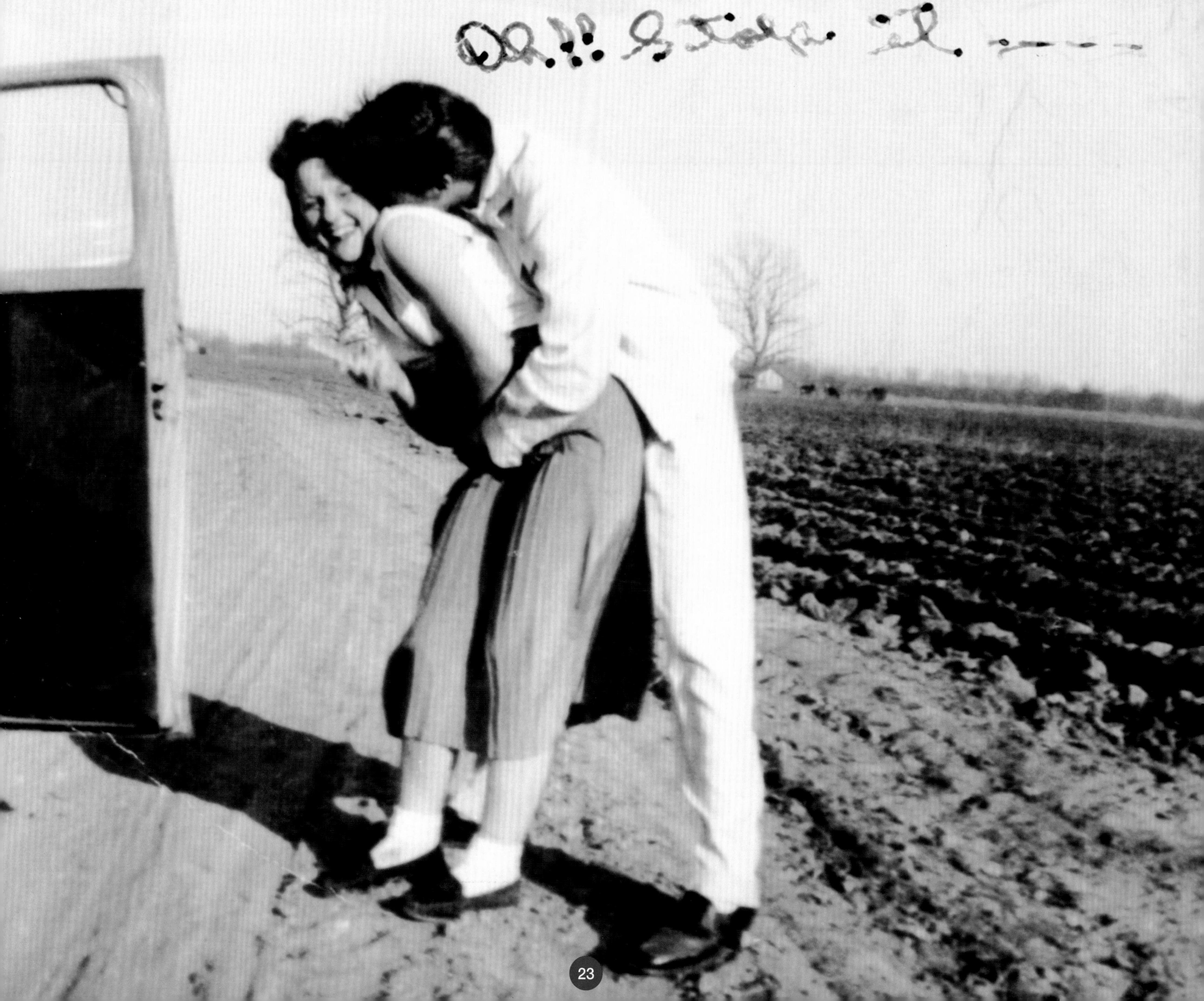

"THAT'S ALL RIGHT"

It was about this time that Sam Phillips had a hillbilly group trying to get its foot in the recording door, the Starlight Wranglers. The group was led by a 22-year-old with the most unlikely hillbilly name ever — Winfield Scott Moore III — who, thankfully, went by Scotty. The Wranglers had recorded a couple of songs for Phillips and Sun, but nothing that made anyone stand up and take notice.

Phillips still had that nagging notion about Elvis, though, and asked Moore to invite Elvis over to his apartment, jam with him and let him know what he thought. On Sunday, July 4, 1954, Moore made the call to Elvis, and the kid came over to play and sing with Moore and the Wranglers' bass player, Bill Black. Nothing really made bells clang, but both

Moore and Black were smitten with something about Elvis' voice. They told Phillips, and he arranged for a studio session with Moore, Black and Elvis the very next night.

As sessions go, it was a dud at first. Nothing much was working, nothing was clicking, and the producer brooded in the control booth while the youngsters played on in the studio. Then during a break, something popped into Elvis' head — a song by an old blues singer named Arthur "Big Boy" Crudup. The song was called "That's All Right."

(Below) Phillips asked Scotty Moore and Bill Black, members of a band called the Starlight Wranglers, to jam with Elvis to see what they thought. (Opposite page) They weren't too impressed, but Phillips arranged a studio session anyway, telling Moore, "Just you and Bill come over, just something for a little rhythm. No use making a big deal out of it."

"All of a sudden," Moore recounted years later, "Elvis just started singing this song, jumping around and acting the fool, and then Bill picked up his bass and he started acting the fool, too, and I started playing with them."

In the booth, Phillips took notice as well. This was the sound he had been looking for, that mix of "race" music and hillbilly that would appeal to the white audience he knew was out there. He told the boys to start over doing the same thing and began recording.

That Wednesday, Phillips made a call to the wildly popular Memphis disc jockey, Dewey Phillips. After his show was over that night at midnight, Dewey went over to meet with Sam and listen to this new sound. After many hours, several beers and a bit of Jack Daniels, both went home impressed. The next night on his show, Dewey Phillips played the new song over and over, and the phone lines lit up. Elvis went to the station to be interviewed — with Dewey making it a point to ask him what high school he attended, thus establishing this was a local talent.

"That's All Right" — soon to be backed by a bigger sensation, "Blue Moon Over Kentucky," a cover of an old Bill Monroe tune — was a hit, and a star was born.

(Preceding page) Elvis was nervous throughout that first studio session and nothing the trio or Phillips tried was working very much, but Elvis had one more song to try. (Below) That song, "That's All Right," was exactly what Phillips was looking for. "It just really flipped Sam," Moore said. "He felt it really had something." (Right) The song and its B side "Blue Moon of Kentucky" were hits on Memphis radio, and soon Elvis and the boys were playing local clubs such as the Eagle's Nest and the Bon Air Club.

"THIS BOY IS NOT BAD"

Later that month, Elvis, Moore and Black performed twice at a rowdy Memphis club called the Bon Air to promote their record. They weren't received with great enthusiasm, but they were on their way. Moore and Black quit the Starlight Wranglers and, along with Elvis, formed Elvis Presley and the Blue Moon Boys. Their first billed gig would be at the Overton Park Shell as a warm-up act to Slim Whitman.

Elvis and the others were a jangle of nerves before they were to go on. "I was scared stiff," Elvis later admitted. Never before had they played before a crowd that big in that big a venue. Elvis gripped the microphone so hard, his knuckles were white. But they were getting paid.

Then the band struck up "That's All Right" and Elvis began doing some of the gyrations he would soon become famous for. Some of it had to do with nerves, some of it with the clothes he was wearing.

(Left and preceding page) Elvis Presley and the Blue Moon Boys, as Elvis, Moore and Black were now calling themselves, continued to play at Memphis venues before being booked to play at the Grand Ole Opry.

"With those old loose britches we wore," explained Moore to Guralnick in *Last Train to Memphis*, "there was lots of material and pleats — well, you shook your leg and it looked like all hell was going on there."

Elvis at first thought the crowd was making fun of him, but when he came off the stage, the manager told him "they was hollering because I was shaking my legs. I went out for an encore and did a little more, and the more I did, the wilder they went."

Though the trio continued to hold full-time jobs, the Blue Moon Boys got more and more gigs, and then, thanks to the prodding of Sam Phillips, they got the biggest one of them all, a spot on The Grand Ole Opry.

The boys were booked to do one song on the Hank Snow segment of the show Saturday, Oct. 2, 1954, and would perform their hit, "Blue Moon Over Kentucky." Elvis sang, and the performance was met with limited response. At first blush, it was an utter disappointment.

But after it was over, Bill Denny, the irascible manager of the Opry, went up to Sam Phillips, who had driven the trio over to Nashville from Memphis. According to many subsequent accounts, Denny supposedly told Phillips that Elvis should go back to driving a truck.

But according to Phillips, that wasn't what Denny said at all.

"This boy is not bad," Denny said and then repeated: "This boy is not bad."

As time would prove, the boy, Elvis, was indeed not bad, not bad at all.

(Left) Elvis' star was growing, albeit slowly, but it wouldn't be long before he was one of the most recognized names in music. (Opposite page) Phillips knew that the chemistry between Elvis and the Blue Moon Boys was a big part of their appeal, but it was Elvis who would connect with the fans.

FROM FARM CLUB TO FAN CLUBS

Even before Elvis and the boys hit the stage at the Grand Ole Opry, Sam Phillips had put them through their paces looking for another record to put out. After all, they couldn't ride just two songs forever.

Once again, it was at the end of a long session that they hit on another that would be a smash. It was a cover of another old blues song, "Good Rockin' Tonight." Like "That's All Right," it was one of those things that just seemed to happen, one of those things that had more to do with feel than anything else. Phillips could feel it, too, could feel they were close to making a major breakthrough.

Phillips kept urging Elvis to go back and do what he had done before. According to Marion Keisker and the biographer Peter Guralnick, Elvis would reply to Phillips, "What did I do? What did I do?" And according to Keisker, Elvis simply didn't know because "it was all so instinctive."

At any rate, the Blue Moon Boys had a little more in their portfolio, which helped Phillips in his quest to break through that barrier that had been erected by more traditional blues and hillbilly purists. He was certain that if he could break that barrier, the sky was the limit.

As Elvis' popularity grew, crowds of screaming girls began to be a normal feature of every tour stop.

"Rock and roll music, if you like it, and you feel it, you can't help but move to it. That's what happens to me. I have to move around. I can't stand still. I've tried it, and I can't do it."

— *Elvis Presley*

(Above) Elvis and the Blue Moon Boys left Memphis headed for Shreveport after getting a booking on The Louisiana Hayride, a radio show on KWKH. They missed a turn at Greenville, Mississippi, supposedly laughing too hard at one of Black's jokes, but eventually arrived in Shreveport, nervous but anxious to play in front of Hayride audiences in 3,200-seat Municipal Auditorium.

THE LOUISIANA "FARM CLUB"

After the Opry gig Oct. 2, 1954, Phillips went to work on the people at the Louisiana Hayride, a radio program on KWKH out of Shreveport, while the boys continued to work Friday nights at clubs in Memphis. The people in Nashville liked to put down the Hayride as "our farm club," but the fact of the matter was that the Hayride was a very big deal indeed. Even if it was a "farm club," such things worked just as in baseball. Players came from AAA to achieve stardom in the big leagues, and Shreveport was the place where such future megastars as Hank Williams, Kitty Wells, Webb Pierce and Jim Reeves had made their debuts. Elvis would be the next.

Elvis, Scotty Moore and Bill Black were booked to do two sets Oct. 16, which happened to be a very good Saturday to be doing such a gig. KWKH was a 50,000-watt station that could be heard at night in 28 states, and on the third Saturday of every month, CBS Radio picked up the show for distribution to more than 190 stations around the country. This was the third Saturday in October.

(Below) It was at the Hayride that Elvis first met the Jordanaires, a quartet who had done backup work for Eddy Arnold. Elvis shyly asked if the Jordanaires would work with him, that is if he ever became as famous as Eddy Arnold.

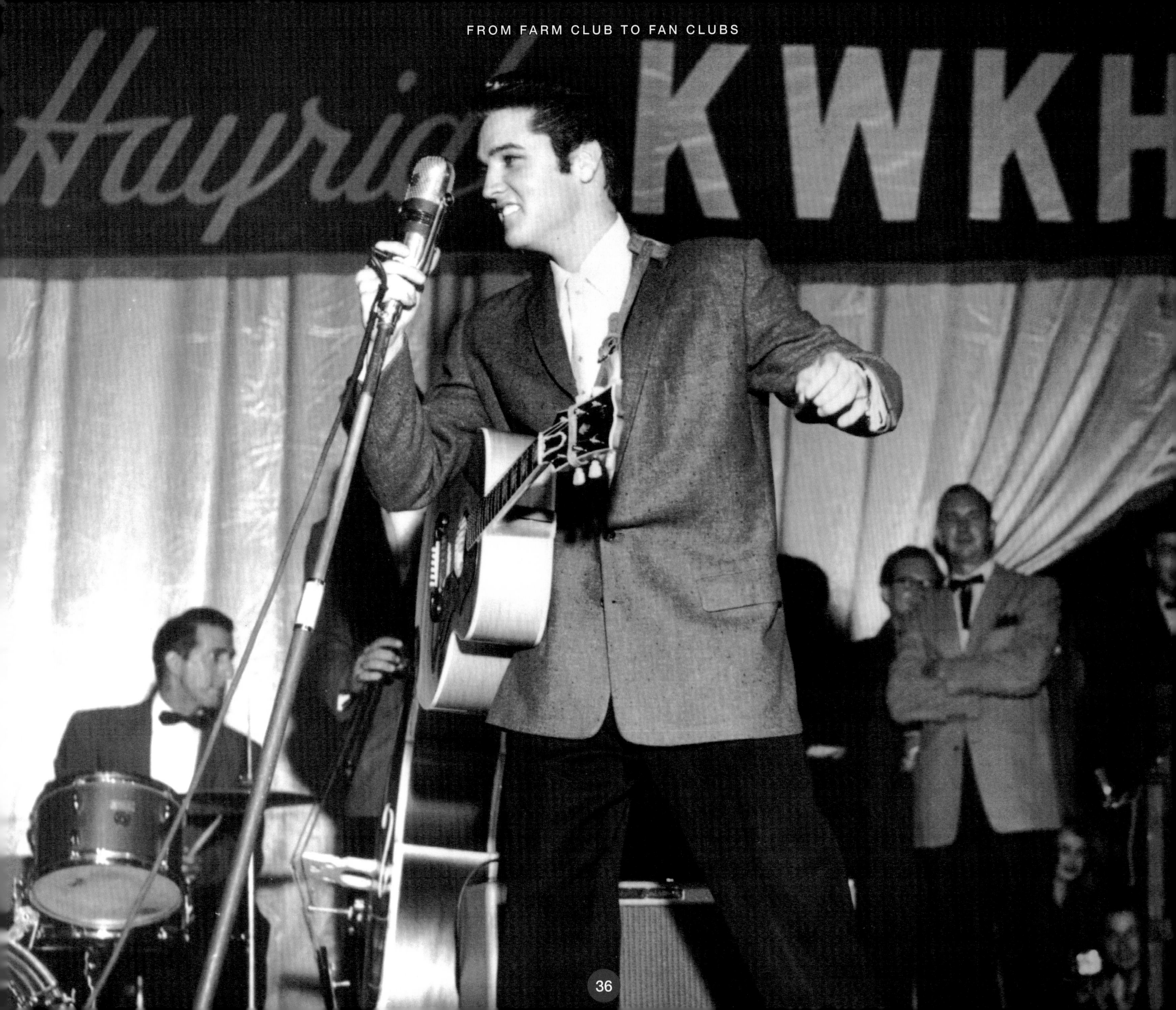
KWKH

As Elvis prepared to go on for his first set, he was noticeably frightened, as "scared stiff" as he had been that night at Overton Park. Sam Phillips was equally nervous as he went to take his seat in the auditorium, a venue bigger than Ryman Auditorium, the home of the Opry. Phillips' worries were made even worse after the first set when the nervous Elvis received only a mild response. Between sets, Phillips tried to calm the youngster down, and others backstage urged him to just "let it all go."

Let it go he did. It helped that the crowd for the second set was younger; part of audience was from a college in Texarkana where Elvis' first record had been a huge hit. The students were on their feet from the time Elvis hit the stage the second time, but they weren't the only ones. A corpulent lady sitting next to Sam Phillips struggled to her feet and hooted the whole time.

"Man," the lady asked Sam, "have you ever heard anything that good?"

(Preceding page and right) Elvis impressed Hayride audiences with his energy and his hip-shaking dance moves.

That was the thing about Elvis. He had a unique sound, to be sure, but it was his connection with the audiences that really put him over the top.

Roy Orbison, yet another soon-to-be legend, saw Elvis in Odessa, Texas, and later told one writer, "His energy was incredible, [and] his instinct was just amazing. I just didn't know what to make of it. There was just no reference point in the culture to compare to it."

MAROONED IN SHREVEPORT

After the Hayride experience, the trio's confidence was soaring to the point where all three quit their day jobs to concentrate on their music, something Vernon Presley did not entirely approve of. Two weeks later, they signed on with the Louisiana Hayride for a year. Elvis would get $18 a show; Moore and Black would get $12.

They went to Shreveport and stayed in a little motel, but some of the extra jobs they thought they were going to get were not coming, and according to Moore, they were beginning to feel "marooned." To the rescue rode Pappy Covington, the booking agent for Hayride, who had a lot of connections in the music business, especially in Texas.

The boys first went to Gladewater, Texas, to meet a man named Tom Perryman, a friend of Covington's who booked acts in the Northeast Texas honky-tonks and hoedowns. Elvis began to find regular work — and new fans. Then, a DJ in Houston, Biff Collie, got him some gigs in the big city. Elvis was even able to send money back to his parents in Memphis, telling them in a telegram, "Here's some money to pay bills. I'll send more next week."

As more and more people became Elvis fans (left), he began playing more shows outside of the Hayride, including the Big Jamboree (opposite page) in Dallas in September 1955.

By this point in time, the group had a new manager, Bob Neal, a Memphis disc jockey on WMPS. Until that time, Moore had been the manager, but he really didn't have much experience in such things. Neal did, having worked with acts within range of his home station in Memphis.

Neal worked his connections and got the group gigs around that part of the South, places like Clarksdale and Corinth, Mississippi, and eventually, a coming-home concert at Ellis Auditorium in Memphis. Elvis had only fourth billing on the card, but as the returning hometown hero, it would seem like top billing. Neal was also working on another very big deal, a tour with country superstar Hank Snow, which would have to be arranged with Snow's wily manager.

His name was Colonel Tom Parker.

Elvis poses with figures of his past, present and future in 1956, left to right, Bob Neal, Sam Phillips, RCA attorney Coleman Tily and Colonel Tom Parker, who was managing country star Hank Snow but saw the potential to make Elvis more than just a regional star.

THE COLONEL TAKES COMMAND

Parker claimed to have been born in West Virginia, but wasn't. He really was born in the Netherlands, but when he moved to the United States and at what age really isn't known. What was known is he was a hustler. He worked in the circus and in carnivals in the South, for the Humane Society and ran a pet cemetery in Florida. The Sunshine State was also where he got his feet wet in the country music waters, promoting the Florida tours of Roy Acuff and Gene Austin and the movie cowboy, Tom Mix.

Singer Eddy Arnold described Parker in his autobiography, *It's a Long Way from Chester County*, "A lot of times people think they're dealing with a rube. 'Oh, I can take him,' they decide. But they don't take him. He's ahead of 'em before they even sit down across the table."

He was ahead of Sam Phillips and Bob Neal, that much is certain now. Phillips didn't like Parker, primarily because he kept putting down Sun Records, saying Elvis needed a bigger record company to take him to the national stage. Phillips didn't have to like it, but the Colonel was right. He and Neal had taken Elvis just about as far as they could, which was to make him a regional phenomenon.

41

Elvis needed a national stage, and he soon would get it.

But first, he had to hit the road with Hank Snow and other acts, including the Carter Family and Hank's son, Jimmie Rodgers Snow. The tour started in Roswell, New Mexico, and wound through Texas and other Southern stops before Elvis made his first trip above the Mason-Dixon Line, to Cleveland, Ohio.

As the tour wound on, a curious thing began to develop. Even though Elvis was on the undercard, he was the top draw. He was churning out that special energy that made him, well, Elvis, and no one wanted to follow that. The women, especially, were smitten with Elvis.

"Grandmas were dancing in the aisles," Jimmie Rodgers Snow said in a 1972 interview.

HITTING BIG WITH "HEARTBREAK"

After another recording session in Memphis — where Elvis cut another hit, "Baby, Let's Play House" — Parker sent Snow, Elvis and the rest out on tour again, this time to 20 spots around the South. It began in New Orleans on May 1, the day after "Baby, Let's Play House" was released. The tour continued through the Deep South and eventually made its way to Jacksonville, Florida.

Elvis' notoriety was growing by the day. At a show in Jacksonville, Florida, Elvis innocently said "Girls, I'll see y'all backstage." By the time he reached the dressing room, girls were tumbling through an open overhead window, and Elvis retreated to the showers, perching atop one of the stalls.

The Colonel "had dollar marks in his eyes" as he witnessed the scene, thought his publicist Mae Axton.

Elvis' crowds were getting bigger and bigger (preceding page), and Elvis sometimes underestimated just how popular he was. Once in Florida, he made an off-hand remark on stage about meeting girls after the show and he was mobbed backstage. Mae Axton, Colonel Parker's publicist, found him huddled on top of a shower stall looking sheepish, as if to say "What did I do?"

Elvis would parlay his musical success into a movie career, working on numerous films with director Hal Wallis (right).

Elvis gets a kiss from his mother after signing a contract with RCA records in 1955. Also pictured are Parker, Vernon Presley, RCA attorney Tily and Bob Neal.

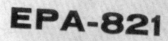

HEARTBREAK HOTEL • I WAS THE ONE • MONEY
HONEY • I FORGOT TO REMEMBER TO FORGET

EPA-821

ELVIS
PRESLEY
HEARTBREAK
HOTEL

Things started moving quickly. After a brief vacation back in Memphis, Elvis and the boys — a drummer, D.J. Fontana, had been added — went back on the road, a trip that included another near-riot in Jacksonville. All the while, Bob Neal and Phillips were fending off buyout offers from other recording companies. Then Parker made his move, and by Aug. 15, 1955, he had Elvis under contract. By Nov. 21, 1955, Parker had negotiated a deal with RCA records for the unprecedented sum of $40,000, buying out Sam Phillips and giving Elvis $5,000 for back royalties.

In the midst of all this financial wheeling and dealing, Mae Axton persuaded Elvis to listen to a song she had written, one she told him would be a million-record seller. Elvis listened to the tune several times and finally said, "That's gonna be my first record."

It was "Heartbreak Hotel."

RCA's first move with Elvis was to re-release some of the old Sun records the company had bought from Phillips.

Things were moving very fast, and it's a wonder the train stayed on the track. On Jan. 10, 1956, Elvis had his first recording session — Chet Atkins on guitar and Floyd Cramer on piano joined the quartet — with RCA, and the first song was, as promised to Axton, "Heartbreak Hotel." By April, it was the No. 1 song in the nation. By the end of the year, Elvis would have an astounding

(Preceding page) Shortly after Elvis signed his contract with RCA, Mae Axton played him a song she had written, a little ditty called "Heartbreak Hotel." Elvis loved it; "Hot damn, Mae, play it again," he said. The song would eventually become his first RCA single. (Right) Elvis shows off a new guitar, a 1955 Martin D-28 with a tooled leather cover that had his name across the bottom.

four No. 1 hits — "I Want You, I Need You, I Love You," "Don't Be Cruel/ Hound Dog" and "Love Me Tender" in addition to "Heartbreak Hotel." Even more incredible was, if you added them all up, Elvis songs were No. 1 on the *Billboard* charts for 25 weeks from April to the end of the year. Just for good measure, his first RCA album "Elvis Presley," released in March, stayed at No. 1 for 10 weeks.

WORKING THE SMALL SCREEN

The record sales were all well and good, but Parker wanted more. That meant television, which was the hottest medium in the country now that TV sets were becoming more and more affordable.

Ed Sullivan was the biggest thing going in '56 with Steve Allen not far behind. Parker settled instead on "Stage Show," which was hosted by the Dorsey Brothers, Jimmy and Tommy, of big-band fame. Their show, which was a lead-in to "The Jackie Gleason Show," was on shaky ground, but apparently that didn't matter. It was network television.

Parker began booking Elvis on the era's biggest TV shows, including the "Milton Berle Show," the "Steve Allen Show" and (above) the "Ed Sullivan Show." (Right) Elvis had another smash hit with "Don't Be Cruel" and its B side, "Hound Dog," a Big Mama Thornton song that Elvis picked up from watching Freddie Bell and the Bellboys do it in their live act. (Opposite page) The Jordanaires accompany Elvis on the "Ed Sullivan Show."

RCA VICTOR
47-6604

ELVIS PRESLEY SINGS

Don't Be Cruel
c/w Hound Dog!

RCA VICTOR
A "New Orthophonic" High Fidelity Recording
ELVIS
ESLEY

Elvis made six straight Saturday night appearances with the Dorsey Brothers, and while it wasn't an unmitigated success, it was a start. It was pleasing enough to Steve Sholes, his handler at RCA, who wrote to Parker, who was on tour:

"He is very hot material here in New York, and with any luck at all, we should do very well."

By the end of March, "Heartbreak Hotel" was closing in on one million copies sold, uncharted territory at the time. Elvis was, as a *Billboard* headline proclaimed, "Hot as a $1 Pistol."

At the end of March, 1956, Elvis headed to the West Coast for a guest appearance on "The Milton Berle Show," which was a step up from "Stage Show." He would do his segment from the deck of the USS Hancock in front of an audience of sailors and their dates.

But just before his appearance with Berle, Parker scheduled a screen test for Elvis by director Hal Wallis using scenes from his upcoming movie, "The Rainmaker." Elvis impressed the director enough for Wallis to offer a three-picture deal to the young singer. It had worked for the likes of Rudy Vallee, Bing Crosby and Frank Sinatra. Why not Elvis, the hottest singer in the land?

(Preceding page) Elvis and the Jordanaires, with Bill Black at far left, perform a skit on the "Milton Berle Show" in 1956. (Above) Elvis would receive large amounts of public criticism for his sexually suggestive performance of "Hound Dog," but Uncle Miltie reportedly told Elvis to leave his guitar backstage and "Let 'em see you, son."

ROCKING THE RATINGS

In the midst of some more touring, the Colonel booked a two-week engagement in Las Vegas, a harbinger of things to come. It wasn't exactly a rousing success — after all, a bunch of middle-age gamblers didn't really constitute his main core audience. But Elvis was pleased.

"Man, I really like Las Vegas," he told one reporter. "I'm going back there the first chance I get."

It should be noted, too, that while this wild ride was going on, Elvis had kept his promise to his parents. He bought them a new house in an upscale neighborhood in Memphis, and they rode around in a new Cadillac. Presumably, he also paid their bill at the grocery store, just as he had said he would as a little kid in Tupelo.

(Preceding page) Elvis' first appearance in Las Vegas was at the New Frontier Hotel, where he did a two-week stint in April of 1956. (Below) Elvis made good on his promise to his mother and bought Cadillacs for himself and his parents, most notably the pink and white vehicle that has come as much a symbol of Elvis as anything.

He went back to New York for another appearance with Milton Berle, and it brought down the house — and the ratings up. For the first time, Berle beat "Sgt. Bilko" in the ratings.

But there were rumblings in the press about Elvis' act. Many called it obscene. One writer called it "grunt and groin," and another called it a "strip tease with clothes on."

Elvis was pressured to respond, and he appeared on a TV show in New York and said, "Rock and roll music, if you like it, and you feel it, you can't help but move to it. That's what happens to me. I have to move around. I can't stand still. I've tried it, and I can't do it."

Elvis did several more TV appearances, including the "Steve Allen Show," while continuing to tour (preceding page and left). (Above) Elvis would soon move from the small screen to the big screen, shooting his first movie, "Love Me Tender," in late '56.

But the folks at NBC were aware of the uproar Elvis was causing, and that led to the disaster that was the appearance on the "Steve Allen Show." Allen, a fine musician in his own right, didn't much care for the new rock 'n' roll, but Elvis was as hot as anyone had ever been and he was booked. What transpired was ridiculous. He put Elvis in white tie and tails and had him sing "Hound Dog" to a basset hound wearing a top hat. Elvis would later refer to that moment as the most ridiculous performance of his career.

Allen, though, had reason to be happy; his show had beaten Ed Sullivan in the ratings for the first time. And Elvis could find a silver lining, too. The Jordanaires — who would back him through the 1960s — made their first appearance with him.

Then there were three shows with Ed Sullivan, and the first drew a record television audience. But on the third, the cameras would only show him from the waist up. Even though Sullivan contended Elvis was a "real decent, fine boy," the networks were very leery of the kid from Memphis.

Elvis had his own parting shot for New York, according to Ernst Jorgensen in *Elvis Presley: A life in music:* "You know, those people in New York ain't gonna change me none."

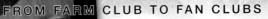

ELVIS IN HOLLYWOOD

Elvis continued to tour and then, in August, headed to Hollywood where he would begin filming his first movie. The deal had been struck by the Colonel the last time they had been on the West Coast — three pictures with escalating salaries of $100,000, $125,000 and $150,000. The original title of the movie was to be "The Reno Brothers," but after the success of Elvis' song "Love Me Tender," Parker pressured to have the title changed. Paramount Pictures agreed. It would debut in mid-November, just in time for the lucrative Thanksgiving and Christmas holidays.

(Left) In "Love Me Tender," Elvis stars as Clint Reno, a man who marries his brother's old girlfriend while his brother fights in the Civil War. (Opposite page) Elvis goes over the lyrics to "Let Me," one of the songs featured on the film's soundtrack, with director Robert D. Webb.

The movie was a huge success at the box office because of one thing — Elvis Presley. A young audience — typically mostly female — would arrive shrieking and pack the movie houses. They would walk out of the theater weeping after seeing Elvis' character, Clint Reno, get murdered at the end.

By the hectic standards of 1956 — contracts, recording sessions, TV appearances, Las Vegas, his first movie — the year 1957 would be practically calm.

Elvis did make one major move, from his house at 1034 Audubon Drive to Graceland, a recently purchased estate south of Memphis that featured a colonial-style mansion built by Dr. Thomas Moore. Elvis redecorated the interior — in an often eclectic style — put up a fieldstone wall around the property and installed music-themed wrought iron gates.

In addition to the new house, there were another four No. 1 hits — "Too Much," "All Shook Up," "Teddy Bear" and "Jailhouse Rock" — and another 25 weeks atop the *Billboard* charts at No. 1. There were two more movies for Hal Wallis and Paramount, "Loving You" and "Jailhouse Rock."

"Loving You" was particularly pleasing to Elvis at the time, because his parents were in it as extras — members of an audience in the movie. "Jailhouse Rock" received the best reviews to that point, primarily because of the rousing dance scene to the title song.

Yes things were good, very good, and Elvis was about to begin filming yet another movie for Wallis, "King Creole," with a contract for seven more.

(Left) Elvis plants a kiss on the cheek of Debra Paget, who played his wife, Cathy Reno, in "Love Me Tender." (Below) Elvis purchased Graceland, a 13-acre estate, in 1957 and promptly moved himself and his parents into the house.

Elvis May Move Into $100,000 Mansion in Whitehaven

(Top) Elvis plays a prisoner whose cellmate, a former country singer, introduces him to the record business in 1957's "Jailhouse Rock." (Right) Elvis' co-star Judy Tyler was killed in a car crash shortly after the movie was finished, and Elvis took the news so hard that he couldn't ever stand to watch the completed film. "Nothing has hurt me as bad in my life," he said.

PVT. ELVIS A. PRESLEY, US53310761

Shooting on "King Creole" began that fall, but in December, Elvis received word from the Selective Service board that he had been drafted into the United States Army.

Paramount had a lot of money — $350,000, a very large sum in that time — in the movie, and Elvis petitioned for a deferment, which was not out of the ordinary, granting someone time to finish a job before reporting. Elvis finished the movie, and on March 24, 1958, he became Pvt. Elvis A. Presley, US53310761.

Elvis could have copped a plea and asked to be assigned to Special Services, that branch that so many entertainers and athletes had joined. That would have allowed him to keep performing with a minimum of real military duty. Elvis, to his eternal credit, chose not to take the easy route. He was inducted into the Army at Fort Chaffee, Arkansas, and was sent to basic training at Fort Hood, Texas. After basic, he was assigned to the 3rd Armored Division and got orders to go to Friedberg, West Germany. Thousands of young girls around the country cried as they viewed the pictures of the army barber sheering Elvis of his celebrated locks.

(Preceding page) In the fall of 1957, Elvis received news that he had been drafted into the U.S. Army, but asked for a deferment so he could finish shooting his latest movie, "King Creole." He reported for duty in March of 1958, losing his famous hair to an Army barber. (Below) Gladys' health had been declining and this is the last picture of the family together before her death in August 1958. Elvis was inconsolable (below right) but shipped out to Germany anyway (right).

He was, by all accounts, a model soldier, neither asking for nor receiving any special treatment. About the only thing that set him apart was he bought an extra set of fatigues for every man in his company and television sets for the base. There were very, very few TV sets on Army bases in Germany in those days.

While in the service, two events transpired that had a profound effect on young Elvis.

The first happened in August 1958. Just before Elvis was to be shipped to Germany, his mother was admitted to the hospital and diagnosed with severe hepatitis. On Aug. 12, Elvis was granted emergency leave to go home to see his beloved mother. Two days later, she died.

Elvis was inconsolable. He wept and mourned his mother. At the funeral, the Blackwood Boys — one of Elvis' and his mother's favorite gospel groups — sang while Elvis sobbed. Later as Gladys' body was lowered into the grave, Elvis cried out:

"Good-bye, my darling, good-bye. You know how much I lived my life just for you. Oh, God! Everything I have is gone."

A few weeks later, Elvis and 1,360 other soldiers boarded troop trains for New York where they boarded a troop ship and set sail for Bremerhaven, West Germany.

It was while serving in Friedberg that Elvis would have another profound moment. At a party in Bad Nauheim, he met a 14-year-old girl.

Her name was Priscilla.

(Left) In just a few short years since the release of "That's All Right" in 1954, Elvis had become a huge sensation. It remained to be seen whether his fame would endure throughout his stint in the Army.

ELVIS RETURNS HOME

The King of Rock returned from Germany in March of 1960. It had been 17 months since he had been in the United States. He took his first steps at Fort Dix, New Jersey, where he was honorably discharged from active duty as a buck sergeant with three stripes — pretty good for a draftee with only two years in the Army.

When Elvis left Fort Dix, it was a Colonel Tom Parker production all the way. For one thing, Elvis was dressed in a tailored dress blue uniform — most other soldiers would walk out in their standard-issue Class A's — and stepped into a waiting limousine surrounded by military police.

Elvis' Army service sent him to Germany, where he lived in Bad Nauheim, about 30 minutes north of Frankfurt.

"I had never seen so many women in my life. They were yelling. They were screaming. I was just horrified. I thought, 'They are going to kill him.' And they would have if they could have gotten loose, I'm afraid."

— *Grand Ole Opry star Minnie Pearl*

The Colonel had also orchestrated the way home to Memphis. He told the press Elvis and his entourage would be staying in New York City at the Hotel Warwick. With a pack of media in hot pursuit, Elvis' limo somehow managed an escape detour to Trenton. The next morning, he headed to Washington, D.C., where he would board a private railcar hooked to The Tennessean for the ride back to civilian life.

Along the way, fans by the hundreds waited for a glimpse. More often than not, Elvis would dutifully go out on the observation platform and wave to the crowd without saying a word. A couple of times Rex Mansfield, an Army buddy along for the ride home, went out on the platform and waved. No one knew the difference. When the train pulled into Knoxville, there were an estimated 3,000 at the station. And it was still another 11 hours to Memphis. By the time the train pulled into Elvis' hometown, the crowd was down to a couple hundred, thanks to snow and a cold, biting wind.

Upon his arrival in the U.S. for discharge, Elvis lands at McGuire Air Force Base in the midst of a snowstorm, and finds a welcoming committee of, among others, the Colonel and Nancy Sinatra.

Elvis receives a certificate of achievement shortly before he leaves Germany for the U.S.

Still, Elvis couldn't contain his excitement. "If I act nervous, it's because I am. I've been away for such a long, long time," he told a *Memphis Press-Scimitar* reporter.

After greeting the shivering crowd, Elvis was packed into a police squad car driven by an old friend and whisked off to Graceland, the iconic mansion he had bought in 1957.

According to a report in the *Press-Scimitar*, "the gates to Graceland swung open, and … the car sped through it. Then the gates closed. The king was once again back on his throne."

(Preceding page) As Elvis prepared to return home, some of his thoughts must have been with Priscilla Beaulieu (below), the daughter of Air Force Captain Paul Beaulieu. A friend had introduced the two, and they hit it off immediately. "I never dreamed this could happen to me," Priscilla said. "Of course, I've been a Presley fan for years. What teenager isn't?" (Right) Elvis and Colonel Parker pose with a TV that RCA sent to celebrate 50 million record sales. The TV was delivered from McDonald Brothers Wholesale Appliance Distributors in Memphis along with a receipt that had a handwritten addition: "The girls here at the office would love to be invited to Graceland someday soon!"

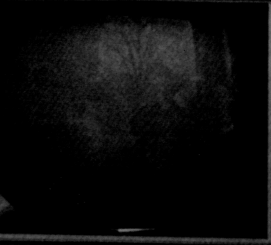

GIVE IT TIME

On the plane ride back to the States and on the train back to Memphis, Elvis had plenty of time to reflect on his life in the Army.

On base, Elvis had been a model soldier, never asking for special treatment, but purchasing extra uniforms for the men in his company. He made friends with many of them and was promoted to PFC, then Specialist 4th Class and, finally, to sergeant.

Off base, however, he was hardly the ordinary Army grunt. His father, Vernon, and his grandmother, Minnie Mae — the latter to do some home-style cooking — came over from Tennessee, and Elvis eventually found a house in Bad Nauheim. He was driven to the base for duty in a black Mercedes. On the weekends, he played touch football with his buddies from his company. And, he often threw parties at the house at 14 Goethestrasse.

It was at one of these parties that he met a young girl named Priscilla Beaulieu, the daughter of an Air Force captain stationed at Wiesbaden. She was sitting in the Eagle Club, which was a community center run by the U.S. Armed Forces for military families, when a volunteer at the club and an acquaintance of Elvis' spotted her. Priscilla was a beautiful young girl, only 14 at the time, but she looked older. The volunteer asked if she was an Elvis Presley fan - of course she was; what teen girl wasn't? - and then asked if she would like to go to a party at Elvis' house in Bad Nauheim. She would.

(Preceding page, left) Vernon and Minnie Mae, Elvis' grandmother, moved to Germany during Elvis' stint in the service to help manage his affairs and, perhaps, provide a little home cooking. (Preceding page, right) Priscilla and Elvis became very close, and though he would have to say goodbye to her in Germany, it wouldn't be long before she would visit him in the States.

At first, her parents balked at the idea, but Capt. Beaulieu eventually relented, allowing her to be chaperoned and home by 11 o'clock. Priscilla went to the party that night, Sept. 13, 1959, wearing a navy-and-white sailor dress with white socks and shoes.

To say love at first sight is almost always an exaggeration, but this time it came close. From their very first visit, Elvis and Priscilla hit it off; and over the next seven months, Elvis saw her as often as he could. He met her parents, who were taken with the polite young man who just happened to be about the biggest star in the world.

Through it all, Priscilla fell deeper in love, and Elvis reciprocated. There would be no intimacies — that would come in time, just give it time.

When the time came for Sgt. Presley to go home, Priscilla was with him at his home in Germany prior to leaving for Rhein-Main Air Base. She rode with him in the car where they said their good-byes, and then while surrounded by Military Police, she watched as they led him to an awaiting plane. When he got to the top of the stairs, he turned to wave at the fans and searched her out, and then waved his last good-bye before entering the plane. Priscilla was then escorted back to the terminal to join her parents.

ELVIS IS BACK WITH PURE MAGIC

All the while Elvis was in the service, the Colonel kept working, kept promoting, albeit in an unusual way. He steadfastly refused to let Elvis perform while in the military, nor would he let him record while in West Germany. His theory, according to Peter Guralnick in the second tome of his Elvis biography, *Careless Love*, was: Keep the commodity scarce and it would be bigger — and more profitable — than ever once Elvis returned to show business.

In the two years Elvis was gone, RCA released several of his songs recorded prior to his departure or done while on leave and one of them, "Big Hunk o' Love," went to No. 1. But while in Germany, there would be no new recordings. The Colonel — and to a point, Elvis himself — were adamant about that.

(Left) Elvis hadn't done any recording while in Germany, but a song he recorded while on leave, "A Big Hunk O' Love," hit it big (opposite page). The musical hiatus wasn't a sign that he was abandoning rock 'n' roll, however. "I will never abandon it as long as people keep appreciating it," he said.

ELVIS PRESLEY

A BIG HUNK O' LOVE

and

MY WISH CAME TRUE

RCA VICTOR
47-7600

A "NEW ORTHOPHONIC" HIGH FIDELITY RECORDING

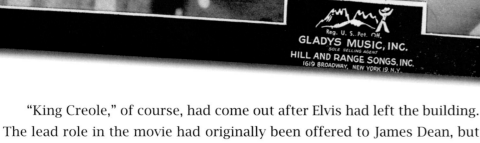

AS LONG AS I HAVE YOU

Words by FRED WISE Music by BEN WEISMAN

Sung by
ELVIS
PRESLEY

as Recorded by
ELVIS PRESLEY
on RCA Victor

IN THE HAL WALLIS PRODUCTION
"KING CREOLE"

A
PARAMOUNT
PICTURE

PRICE
60¢
IN U.S.A.

GLADYS MUSIC, INC.
SOLE SELLING AGENT
HILL AND RANGE SONGS, INC.
1619 BROADWAY, NEW YORK 19, N.Y.

album went as high as No. 2 on the *Billboard* charts. It is generally regarded as one of the best Elvis movies. It was, at least, said to be his personal favorite.

On March 20, he began his triumphant return. The first stop was the recording studio, a session that was attended by just about every high-ranking person in the business. It was a rousing success, and the result was one of his very best albums, "Elvis Is Back!" Among the cuts on the album were some of his finest and most enduring songs such as "It's Now Or Never" and "Are You Lonesome Tonight?"

The critics gushed. One called it "pure magic," and another described Elvis' rendition of "Lonesome" as "natural, unforced, dead in tune and totally distinctive." The album would soar to the top of the charts, of course, but there was something more to it. It was a change in direction, away from some of the earlier, earthier music. Some called it "adult music." Maybe, but there we still plenty of young girls to scream over him.

(Left) "King Creole," Elvis' last movie before his military service, had been a success, the director noting that Elvis "had a great sense of timing; there was great honesty in his acting." (Opposite page) Co-star Walter Matthau agreed. "He was intelligent enough to know what a character was and how to play the character by simply being himself through the means of the story."

LIVING COLOURS

Elvis Unlimited PRODUCTIONS

MIRACLE ✦ PRINTING

ELVIS
IS BACK!

**** THE ****
ULTIMATE
POST ARMY ELVIS BOOK!
Follow Elvis' footsteps through-
out the exciting year 1960.

From his return to US soil at Fort
Dix in March... to the record-
ing of his first sacred album in
Nashville in October.

"King Creole," of course, had come out after Elvis had left the building. The lead role in the movie had originally been offered to James Dean, but after his tragic, deadly accident, the part went to Elvis, and it became a musical with Walter Matthau and Carolyn Jones sharing top billing. The film ranked No. 9 among money-makers for the year, and the soundtrack

Elvis also had a date with Frank Sinatra for a television special, "The Frank Sinatra Timex Show: Welcome Home Elvis Special." This was a bit ironic, given that Sinatra had been harsh in his criticism of Elvis when he first burst on the scene in '56. Elvis had been forgiving then, and later Sinatra would make things right between them. In fact, Sinatra's then-19-year-old daughter, Nancy, had given Elvis a lace white dress shirt he had worn under his dress blues on the train trip home to Memphis. The Sinatra show would, however, be his last television appearance for many years to come.

If there were any doubts Elvis was back, all anyone had to do was check *Billboard*. Three of his new singles — "Stuck on You," "It's Now or Never," "Are You Lonesome Tonight?" — reached the top of the charts in 1960 and stayed there for 15 weeks.

(Preceding page) Elvis, Frank Sinatra and Col. Parker go over sheet music for their duet during rehearsals for Elvis' first TV performance since his return from the service, the "Frank Sinatra Timex Show: Welcome Home Elvis Special." Elvis appeared in his military uniform (above) with Frank and Nancy Sinatra, Sammy Davis Jr. and Joey Bishop, but did part of the show in a tuxedo (right), which he had rented for the occasion.

ACE FORMAL WEAR
1125 West Flagler Street
Miami 36, Florida

267025

Customer's Order No.

DATE MARCH 26, 1960

SOLD TO MR. ELVIS PRESLEY

ADDRESS

SALESMAN _____ TERMS

	CASH	CHARGE	C. O. D.	PAID OUT	RETD. MDSE.	RECD. ON ACCT.
QUAN.	DESCRIPTION				PRICE	AMOUNT
1	TUXEDO				150.00	
3	RENTALS - TUXEDOS @ $25.00 EACH				75.00	
					225.00	
	3% STATE TAX				6.75	
					231.75	
					25.75	
					206.	

ALL Claims and Returned Goods MUST Be Accompanied By This Bill

SIGNA____ SINATRA-TV SHOW

BIG STARS ON THE BIG SCREEN

Though Elvis still topped the charts, his music was becoming almost secondary. There were movies to be made, beginning with 1960's "G.I. Blues." It would be filmed under the direction of Hal Wallis in Hollywood. Once again, the Colonel booked a cross-country train — he had another to Miami to do the Sinatra special — and big crowds were waiting at every whistle stop. The sound track from the movie — another sign of things to come — was another solid No. 1 hit.

Movies would be Elvis' main genre over the next decade — 27 of them, at least two a year. All of them would be moneymakers, if not critical successes. Wallis would say later: "An Elvis Presley movie is the only sure thing in Hollywood."

Elvis made two more movies in '60, neither of which would rank among his favorites. The first was called "Flaming Star" and other was "Wild in the Country." Both were critical duds, but box-office hits. Elvis was also beginning to lure some formidable female co-stars. In "Flaming Star," Delores del Rio, a fiery, sultry star of the '30s and '40s, came out of retirement to make her first movie in nearly 20 years, playing the Indian mother to Elvis' half-breed character. In the second flick, young starlets Tuesday Weld, Hope Lange and Millie Perkins played love interests. Perkins, by the way, broke her arm when she slapped Elvis' character during the shooting.

(Left) Elvis began focusing much more on his movies in 1960, beginning with "G.I. Blues," a tale of an enlisted man falling in love with a club dancer, played by Juliet Prowse. (Opposite page) Elvis takes a punch in "G.I. Blues," talks with a staff member on the set of "Wild In The Country," and cozies up to Barbara Eden while Steve Forrest looks on while on the set of "Flaming Star."

ELVIS SINGS FLAMING STAR

CAMDEN
STEREO

CAS-2304

Wonderful World
Night Life
All I Needed Was the Rain
Too Much Monkey Business
Yellow Rose of Texas
The Eyes of Texas
She's a Machine
Do the Vega
Tiger Man

ELVIS
NOW
WILD IN THE
COUNTRY
A JERRY WALD
PRODUCTION

(Below) Elvis is nearly buried under a pile of leis as he greets fans at the Honolulu airport in 1961. (Opposite page) Elvis announces at a press conference that he will put on a free show to raise money for a memorial at the site of the USS Arizona, which was sunk in the attack on Pearl Harbor.

Big-name stars always seemed to share the billing with Elvis, even if they were not big time at the moment. Debra Paget was the first female of note, followed by Angela Lansbury, Ann-Margret, Raquel Welch, Barbara Stanwyck, Nancy Sinatra, Elsa Lancaster and Mary Ann Mobley, to name a few. Shelley Fabares would appear in three Elvis movies.

While in California doing all this filming, Elvis rented a house from the Shah of Iran and spent much of his time on the West Coast. He made visits back to Memphis and Graceland, but his father had remarried, this time to the ex-wife of a sergeant Vernon had met in West Germany. With the newlyweds — and her three children — ensconced in the mansion, Elvis didn't go home at Christmas because he didn't feel comfortable there.

Because of the time required on the set, Elvis did no touring in those first years after his return, but he did find time to do a few charity concerts at the urging of the Colonel. Two of them were in Memphis and the other was booked for Honolulu. For the final concert in Memphis, Elvis reunited his old musical gang, including Scotty Moore, D.J. Fontana and the Jordanaires. It was a huge success.

THE ARIZONA MEMORIAL

The Colonel had read a story in one of the Los Angeles newspapers lamenting the lack of funds to build a Pearl Harbor Memorial honoring the fallen soldiers and sailors from the Japanese attack on the island Dec. 7, 1941. The people directing the fund drive wanted the memorial at the site of USS Arizona, which had been sunk that day entombing 1,102 sailors, to be completed by the 20th anniversary of the bombing in 1961.

(Above) Elvis performs during the concert at Pearl Harbor's Bloch Arena (above right). (Opposite page) Elvis raised $62,000 for the memorial, kicking in $5,000 from himself and the Colonel. He and the Colonel visited the memorial several years after it was built and left a wreath.

Elvis would be going to Hawaii to begin filming "Blue Hawaii" that year, and Parker, who had served in the Army there, proposed a free concert with all the proceeds going to the memorial fund. If they could get the appropriate arena and make sure the printing of tickets, ushers, etc., were free, Elvis would donate his services.

When Elvis finally arrived in Honolulu on a Pan-Am jet, the scene at the airport was chaotic. Thousands of screaming fans — as usual, most of them young and female — greeted his arrival. "The greeting roared like thunder across Honolulu International Airport," read an account in the *Honolulu Advertiser*. "… as 3,000 teenage fans (and some not so young) greeted their hero."

One of those not impressed was Grand Ole Opry star Minnie Pearl, a member of Elvis' traveling party. "I had never seen so many women in my life," Pearl told Guralnick. "They were yelling. They were screaming. I was just horrified. I thought, 'They are going to kill him.' And they would have if they could have gotten loose, I'm afraid."

To which Elvis replied, "They're not going to hurt me."

The concert itself was a rousing affair. The old Elvis strutted his stuff on stage, belting out one hit after another. According to Guralnick, Jordanaire Gordon Stocker said there "was a spontaneity to the performance that most closely resembled a man being let out of jail."

THE MOVIES KEPT COMING

But soon it would be back to the prison of the movie lot, beginning with "Blue Hawaii," a break from his previous two movies and the start of run of formulaic musical comedies stamped with the Hal Wallis trademark. Whereas in "Flaming Star" there had been only two songs, in "Blue Hawaii" there were 14. Angela Lansbury played Elvis' mother, though in reality she was only 10 years older.

(Preceding page) Elvis was headed to Hawaii even before planning the memorial concert to begin filming "Blue Hawaii," the first of his movies to serve merely as a vehicle for the soundtrack. (Right) The plot revolves around an ex-soldier who ignores his father's advice to go to work at the Great Southern Hawaiian Fruit Company and works instead as a tour guide at his girlfriend's agency. His first tour is a group of school girls, one of which is played by Jenny Maxwell.

"BLUE HAWAII"

A Hal Wallis Production   A Paramount Picture   Panavision®   Technicolor®

The movies kept coming. "Follow That Dream" came after the Hawaii movie. Elvis next played a boxer in "Kid Galahad," a remake of a 1937 movie. Then, it was back to the islands to film "Girls! Girls! Girls!" The movies continued with the same, proven formula. If it ain't broke, don't fix it seemed to be the mantra. "Girls!" earned Elvis his first — and only — Golden Globe nomination. The films had another thing in common: The sound track albums sold like hotcakes.

All this time, Elvis had been in contact with Priscilla back in West Germany, and he invited her to visit him in Memphis. Her parents allowed her to go on the condition she have a chaperone, she would live in separate quarters from Elvis.

The first visit came in June 1962 after numerous calls from Elvis and Vernon persuading Priscilla's parents to let her visit him in Los Angles during the summer school break. After her summer visit, Elvis invited Priscilla to Memphis for Christmas. In 1963 Elvis convinced Priscilla's parents to let her finish school and graduate in Memphis.

(Left) Elvis strapped on boxing gloves for 1962's "Kid Galahad." To prepare for his role, he trained with former junior welterweight champion Mushy Callahan, spent hours on the speedbag and dropped 12 pounds. "He's got a good physique and excellent coordination," Callahan said. "He never boxed before but he picked it up quick because of his karate training." (Opposite page and below) Laurel Goodwin and Elvis in a scene from "Girls! Girls! Girls!" One of Elvis' best songs from this period, "Return to Sender," was featured on the soundtrack album.

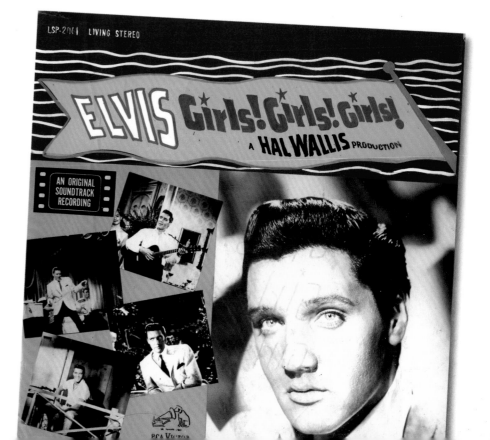

MEETING "THE FAB FOUR"

While the courtship of Priscilla went on, so did the string of movies. Elvis would make two, "Fun In Acapulco" and "It Happened at the World's Fair," in 1963 before making one of his most iconic films the next year.

"Viva Las Vegas," released in 1964, was significant in two respects. One was Elvis' widely reported off-screen romance with co-star Ann-Margret. The other was at the box office. "Viva Las Vegas" remains the highest-grossing Presley movie ever and showed a 500 percent return over the cost of production. Elvis was a big, big star, and he was making big, big money. Enough money to buy Franklin D. Roosevelt's retired yacht, the USS Potomac, for $55,000. Elvis originally planned to donate the ship to the March of Dimes, but the gift was refused so he ended up giving it to St. Judes Children's Hospital.

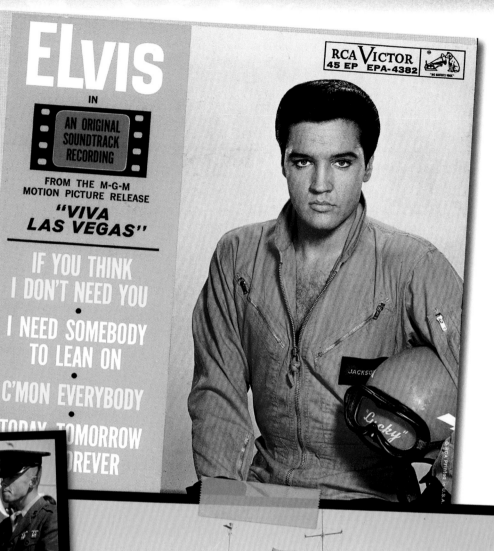

(Preceding page, top) Elvis starred in "Fun In Acapulco" in 1963 with Ursula Andress, the blonde bombshell from the famous bikini scene in James Bond's "Dr. No." (Preceding page, bottom) In "Viva Las Vegas" it was Ann-Margret, playing a swimming pool manager to Elvis' stock car driver. (Below) Elvis purchased the USS Potomac, formerly Franklin D. Roosevelt's floating White House, and donated it to the March of Dimes, which couldn't accept it, so he donated it to St. Judes Children's Hospital instead.

Meanwhile, there was something disturbing going on in the world of music; the whole scene was changing. Suddenly, the Beatles were the main attraction for the screaming teenage girls. It wasn't as though Elvis had quit making records; he hadn't. Some of them were very well received, including one of his favorites, the gospel album "How Great Thou Art."

With the Beatles' success, Parker saw yet another promotional opportunity. He sent wires of congratulations to the group in his and Elvis' names; he sent them gifts. Then he invited Paul, John, George and Ringo to meet Elvis at his new home-away-from-home in Bel Air, California.

As meetings go, it wasn't exactly the roaring success the Colonel and the Beatles' manager, Brian Epstein, had imagined. But Ringo played some pool with two of Elvis' buddies, and Elvis jammed with Lennon and McCartney. Lennon went out of his way to ask Jerry Schilling to tell Elvis that "if hadn't been for him, I would have been nothing."

(Above) Elvis gets roped in on the set of "Tickle Me." (Opposite page) Elvis spent most of the rest of the 1960s working on more movies, such as "Kissing Cousins," "Harum Scarum," "Paradise-Hawaiian Style" and "Clambake." (Opposite page, center right) Elvis' last movie was "Change of Habit," where he had to convince a young Mary Tyler Moore to give up becoming a nun.

Over 830,000 Copies
Sold Every Week

The Australian

May 24, 1967

Registered in Australia for transmission by post as a newspaper.

WOMEN'S WEEKLY

PRICE

15c

New Zealand 1/6 (15c)
New Guinea 33c
Malaysia $1.00

ELVIS AND
HIS BRIDE

RECIPES FOR DIETERS — BOOKLET: CARE OF PETS

(Above and opposite page) Elvis gave up his bachelorhood when he married Priscilla in a small ceremony at the Aladdin Hotel in Las Vegas after visiting the Clark County Courthouse at 3 a.m. to get the license. "She's got everything a man could want in a wife," Elvis told *Weekend* magazine.

THE MAKINGS OF A COMEBACK

If it hadn't been for Elvis, some of the studios might have been nothing, too. Time and time again, his movies came to rescue them from some ill-advised commitments. Hal Wallis admitted to the press in 1964 that, if it hadn't been for the Elvis vehicles such as "Girl Happy" or "Kissing Cousins," some more high-browed — and critically successful — movies such as "Becket" starring Richard Burton and Peter O'Toole might not have been made.

Elvis was aware of the exploitation and many times called the producers and directors out on it. He was taken advantage of again in '65 when his movie "Tickle Me" — generally regarded as one of his weakest — helped Allied Artists stay away from bankruptcy. Still he continued to add to his list of flicks with "Harum Scarum," "Paradise-Hawaii Style," "Spinout," "Clambake," "Stay Away Joe" and more.

Elvis blamed his "humdrum movies" for his decline in popularity in the late '60s, wrote Priscilla in her autobiography *Elvis and Me*. He "loathed their stock plots and short shooting schedules."

He had long wanted to be taken seriously as an actor, and many thought he could be. Even Wallis had thought that back when Elvis first stepped in front of the cameras for "Love Me Tender" in 1956. But that chance never came. He made his last movies in 1969, "Charro!" — his only non-singing role — "The Trouble With Girls" and "Change of Habit" with Mary Tyler Moore, but none had the serious role he was looking for.

Elvis did get serious about one thing in his life. He proposed to Priscilla at Christmas 1966 and married her the next May in a suite at the Aladdin Hotel in Las Vegas. It was a small ceremony with only family and a few friends present. "Our little girl is going to be a good wife," said Colonel Beaulieu. She would soon be both wife and mother, when their daughter, Lisa Marie, arrived Feb. 1, 1968.

Elvis was happy as a new father but longed for a return to the musical stage instead of the sound stage. In 1968 Elvis would return to what he really loved, performing to live audiences.

He would launch a comeback.

(Left) Elvis' run through Hollywood was coming to an end and he was anxious to get back to performing in front of live audiences, rather than the characters he often played in the movies (opposite page).

CHOSEN TO BE ELVIS PRESLEY

By the end of the 1960s, Elvis Presley had become increasingly aware the musical scene had been passing him by. It wasn't just the Beatles, there were a host of others — the Rolling Stones, Jefferson Airplane, The Doors, Janis Joplin, the Grateful Dead, the list could go on and on.

Elvis' decline as a singer was noticeable on the *Billboard* charts. Though his soundtrack albums continued to sell, he had not had a No. 1 hit in the States since 1962. Since then, only six of his singles had even cracked the top 10.

Colonel Parker could read the handwriting on the wall. Parker had put in motion plans for Elvis' return to television, a medium he hadn't touched since his Frank Sinatra special back in 1960.

(Preceding page) Elvis returned to the live stage in 1968 for a TV special that came to be known as the 1968 Comeback Special. (Above) Dressed in black leather with his hair swept back, Elvis once again looked like the King of Rock.

"There are several unbelievable things about Elvis, but the most incredible is his staying power in a world where meteoric careers fade like shooting stars."

— *Newsweek*

FINDING HIS WAY BACK HOME

The Colonel negotiated a deal with NBC for an hour-long special to be aired in December. It was called simply "Elvis," though fans and critics later would call it the '68 Comeback Special. While some of the segments of the show were stage productions, some of it was also performed before a small live audience, something Elvis hadn't done since that benefit in Hawaii in 1961. He dressed in black leather and played his guitar and exuded an uninhibited energy no one had seen for a long, long time.

"There is something magical about watching a man who has lost himself find his way back home," Jon Landau wrote in the short-lived, campy Hearst magazine, *Eye*. "He sang with the power people no longer expect of rock-and-roll singers."

The special, which aired Dec. 3, 1968, was a smash. It was NBC's highest-rated show of the season, and the album from it moved into the top 10. The star was elated and as high on his career as he had been in years. The King of Rock was back. Again.

"He was out of prison, man," said Jerry Schilling, one of the entourage who would go on to a successful career of his own as a manager and later would work with Elvis' daughter, Lisa Marie.

He had also managed to slip the clutches of the Colonel, if only ever so slightly. Parker had originally wanted the show to be all Christmas songs, but Elvis and director Steve Binder had a different perspective.

He didn't win much from Parker. According to many sources, Elvis had grown apart from the man. But, as Priscilla pointed out in *Elvis and Me*, Elvis "detested the business side of [his career]. He would sign a contract without even reading it."

Elvis biographer Peter Guralnick probably summed up the relationship between Elvis and Parker best when he said:

(Left) Some parts of the comeback special were pre-recorded, including a bordello scene that was later cut because of the show's sponsor, Singer.

The two "were really like, in a sense, a married couple," he wrote, "who started out with great love, loyalty and respect which lasted for a considerable period of time, and went through a number of stages until, towards the end of Elvis' life, they should have walked away. None of the rules of the relationship were operative any longer, yet neither had the courage to walk away, for a variety of reasons."

(Right) Elvis did do several sets on a small stage surrounded by audience members during the 1968 television special. (Below) Alan Fortas, the Colonel, Lamar Fike, Joe Esposito and Charlie Hodge join Elvis on the set of the '68 special.

101

VIVA LAS VEGAS

At any rate, Elvis was headed in a direction far different from the one which he had traveled since he got out of the Army. He wasn't a movie prop any more; he was back to being a singer and an entertainer.

After the special, Elvis went back to the studio to record. Those sessions led to two hugely successful and critically lauded albums, "From Elvis in Memphis" and "From Memphis to Vegas/Vegas to Memphis," which was a double album. The recordings yielded such hit singles as "Suspicious Minds," "In the Ghetto," "Kentucky Rain" and "Don't Cry Daddy." "Suspicious Minds" would be his last *Billboard* No. 1.

Now, Elvis was anxious to return to the stage. After the special, many offers came in from overseas, where he had remained immensely popular — he had three No. 1 hits in the United Kingdom in the middle '60s when he had none in the U.S. The London Palladium offered $28,000 for a one-week stand, to which the Colonel replied, "That's fine for me, now what can you do for Elvis?"

The lack of overseas engagements has remained a mystery. There could have been many factors — lack of large venues, security issues and the inability to pay fees the Colonel wanted.

Instead of a tour, then, Parker booked Elvis into the new International Hotel in Vegas, where he would do 57 shows over four weeks. Elvis was nervous about the gig, recalling his less-than-smashing stint in the city in 1956. Not to worry. Elvis delivered a rollicking opening show and was received warmly by the star-studded audience. He got three standing ovations when it was over.

(Preceding page, bottom) Elvis signs a fake contract at a photo op with officials for the new International Hotel on the hotel's construction site in Las Vegas in February 1969. The Colonel had arranged for a four-week, seven-nights-a-week gig, but the actual contract won't be signed until April. (Preceding page, top left) "From Elvis In Memphis" was released in June 1969 with the top 10 hit "In The Ghetto." (Preceding page, top right) Elvis and Priscilla frequently entertained guests, such as Tom Jones, in their suite at the International after performances.

Newsweek wrote, "There are several unbelievable things about Elvis, but the most incredible is his staying power in a world where meteoric careers fade like shooting stars."

The show was such a success that Parker signed a contract with the hotel to do shows in February and August every year for the next five years. The price tag: $1 million a year.

That Elvis could command such a number could be found in, well, the numbers. For the 57 shows, he attracted more than 100,000 paying customers. The take at the gate alone was $1.5 million. And that didn't count what the fans dropped at the tables. Vegas had never seen anything like it.

"I GUESS I'VE STILL GOT IT"

The new Elvis was tanned and fit for this next stage in his career, something that could be attributed in part to his obsession with karate, a hobby he had first encountered while in the Army. He earned a black belt and eventually would get Priscilla to take up the discipline. He was ready to go back on the road and tour.

(Upper left and left) Elvis happily clowns with Lisa Marie during a family photo session with Priscilla in 1970. (Above) Elvis hired the Sweet Inspirations, a soul quartet that had backed Aretha Franklin, to sing backup on portions of his Vegas shows. (Opposite page, top) Elvis holds a press conference after one of his Vegas shows. (Opposite page, bottom) Elvis squares off with karate master Kang Rhee, whom he studied under for four years in the early '70s.

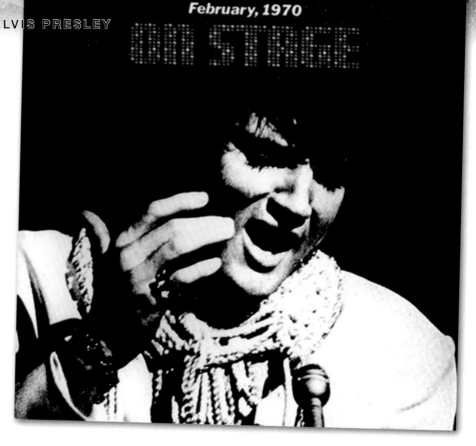

February, 1970
ON STAGE

First, he returned to Las Vegas for his next scheduled gig at the International — eventually renamed the Las Vegas Hilton International — which would run from the end of January through February. Some thought it a mistake to return to The Strip so soon, but he fooled them again, setting attendance records. The stint was recorded on the album "On Stage — February 1970." It was during that gig at the International that Elvis donned a jumpsuit for the first time, forming a picture of the singer now entrenched in the minds of several generations, a picture far removed from the thin, pink-and-black clad kid of the '50s.

Once the Vegas shows were over, he hit the road. The first stop was Houston and the massive Astrodome. Elvis was booked for six shows — three matinees and three evening shows — as the headliner for the Houston Livestock Show and Rodeo. That may sound like a letdown from Las Vegas, but it really wasn't. In Texas, this was a very big deal. It was also, according to Robert Hilburn of the *Los Angeles Times*, a test to see if Elvis still had his grass-roots popularity, in addition to his newfound fame in Vegas.

The Friday night crowd beat the standing record by 10,000, and the Saturday matinee did even better than that. The Saturday night crowd set an attendance record for an indoor rodeo, and overall, the six shows drew more than 200,000 fans. "I guess I've still got it after all," Elvis commented. He did indeed still have it.

(Preceding page, top right) Elvis released a live album, "Elvis On Stage," recorded from his International Hotel performances, in early 1970. (Preceding page, left) He followed that up in November with a documentary called "Elvis — That's The Way It Is," which followed him both in the studio and at his live performances. (Above) Elvis played the Houston Livestock Show and Rodeo in 1970 and for several years after.

ELVIS *That's The Way It Is* Elvis

TROUBLE ON THE HOME FRONT

By August 1970, he was back in Vegas for his second scheduled appearance of the year. After much haggling, the Colonel had arranged for MGM to film rehearsals and some of the shows for a documentary, "Elvis — That's The Way It Is."

While Elvis was doing his thing during his August stint at the International, the Colonel was already plotting a six-city tour, Elvis' first since 1958. It would start in Phoenix and wind up in Mobile, Alabama, Elvis' old stomping ground. His first road trip in a very long time would be a very smooth one.

Elvis had returned to the public consciousness with bang. If he had been lost in the 1960s, he was back in the 1970s. In December 1970, he even had a meeting with President Richard Nixon. A month later, he was honored as one of the 10 outstanding young men in the nation — hard to believe, but Elvis was still only 36 — and in the summer of 1971, the city of Memphis renamed part of the road that runs past Graceland as Elvis Presley Boulevard. He also received a Lifetime Achievement Award from the National Academy of Recording Arts.

(Preceding page, bottom) Elvis rehearses for one of his Vegas shows. (Preceding page, top) Elvis was voted one of the top 10 young men in the nation by the Jaycees in 1970. Here he poses with fellow recipient Boston City Council member Tom Atkins. (Above) Elvis meets with President Richard M. Nixon at The White House in December 1970 to offer his services toward the government's efforts to battle drugs.

Things were going very well, but there was trouble on the home front.

It was February 1972 that Priscilla told Elvis she wanted to leave the marriage. Following a separation they agreed that Elvis should be the one to file divorce papers, concerned about the public reaction.

The main reason for Priscilla leaving wasn't that they didn't care for each other, but for the fact that Elvis was gone too often and often too long. It was for her a loneliness that led to heartbreak. On October 9, 1973, the two legally divorced. It was very amicable, and they remained lovingly close and shared joint custody of little Lisa Marie.

After the separation, Elvis went back to touring — 14 dates including the four-day opener at Madison Square Garden in New York City, which sold out all four days. That had never happened at the Garden before. MGM filmed the whole tour, and the result was a second Elvis documentary, "Elvis on Tour," which would win a 1972 Golden Globe award as the year's best..

While Elvis was touring and doing his Vegas shows, Parker was feverishly working behind the scenes for the next big deal. Working with a group of West Coast promoters, his first idea had been a pay-per-view show from the stadium in Anaheim, California. It would be seen in theaters, not homes, much the same way boxing had begun raking in huge audiences in the'70s.

However, the deal fell through when those who would have to finance it simply could not believe the numbers the Colonel was throwing around. There would be no pay-per-view, but Parker was still working, as always, toward a big — a very big — splash.

It would take a while, but it would come.

(Left) Oct. 9, 1973, Elvis and Priscilla leaving Santa Monica courthouse arm-in-arm after the divorce was final. The two remained friends and shared custody of Lisa Marie. (Opposite page) Elvis, Vernon and the rest of the entourage head for the stage during an unidentified show in the '70s.

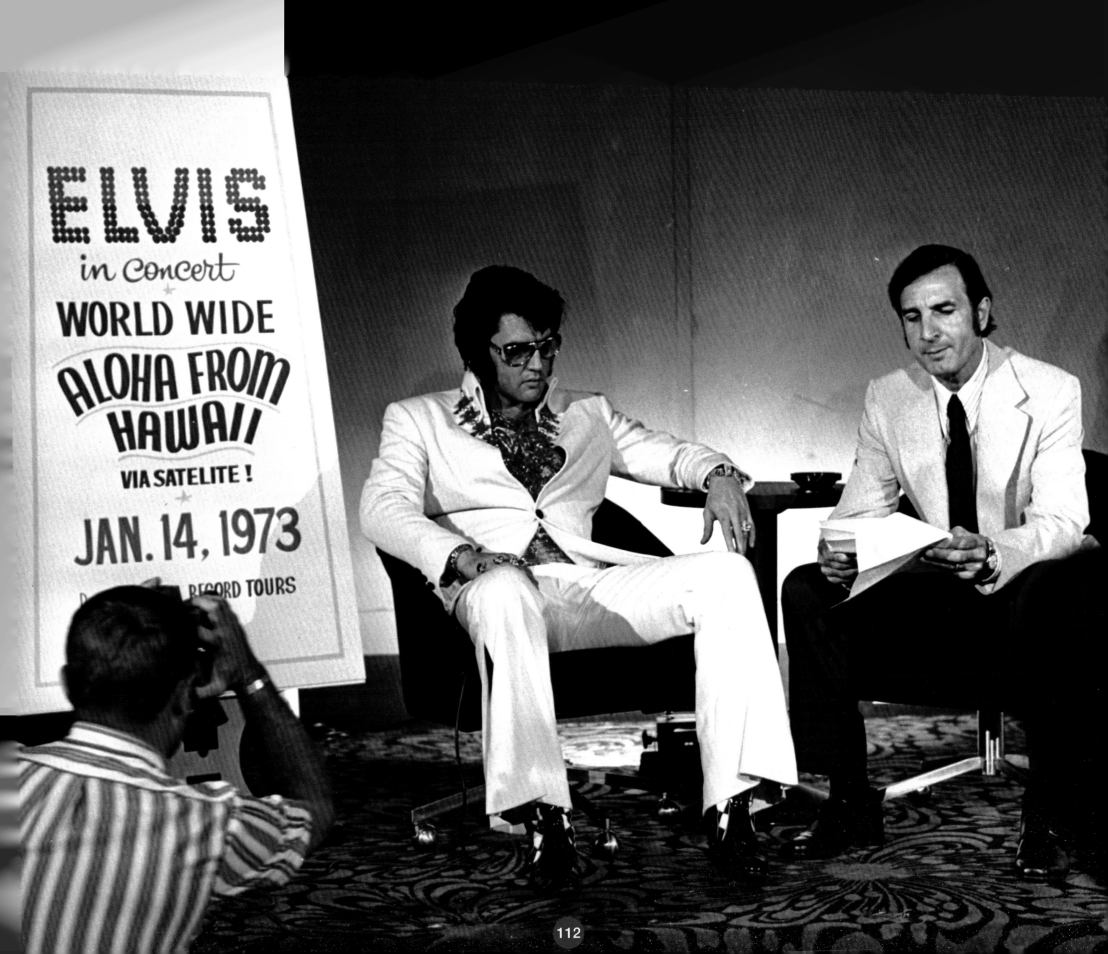

THE "AMERICAN EAGLE"

On Sept. 6, 1972, the last day of that year's engagement at the International, Parker called a press conference between the last two shows. He said there would be a telecast handled by NBC originating in Hawaii in January 1973. It would be simulcast around the world to an estimated 1.5 billion people, an astonishing number. An album would simultaneously released. This was the next big promotion he had been angling for. It would be called "Aloha from Hawaii."

In the meantime, Elvis began dating Linda Thompson after the separation and impending divorce with Priscilla.

Elvis had also become more and more introspective and spiritual as time went on. Perhaps this was to be expected, given his church upbringing and his love for gospel music. It was helped along by his hair stylist Larry Geller.

(Preceding page) Elvis does publicity for his 1973 Aloha From Hawaii concert that was broadcast around the world via satellite. (Right) By that time, Elvis and Priscilla officially divorced, and Elvis was dating Linda Thompson, a Memphis girl whom he had met at the Memphian Theatre.

Elvis began to have deep conversations with Geller about his thoughts and anxieties. Geller told Guralnick for *Careless Love* that his boss told him, "There's got to be a reason … why I was chosen to be Elvis Presley."

Geller gave Elvis books on religion and mysticism, and he read them voraciously; he would take loads of books with him when he toured. He told Geller, "I swear to God, no one knows how lonely I get and how empty I feel."

As the date for the Hawaii extravaganza drew near, Elvis began to get caught up the excitement as well. He wanted a distinctive look for something that everyone was certain would make history. He huddled with his clothes designer, Bill Belew, and the result was the famed "American Eagle" jumpsuit.

"It was one of only three times in all the times we were together he made a request," Belew told Guralnick. "We made an American eagle belt for it, a white leather belt about three or four inches wide with four or five ovals with American eagles on them. And, of course, the cape."

Of course there would be a cape. The cape had become as much of the Elvis look as the jumpsuit and scarves.

(Left and below) Sketches of Elvis' famed jumpsuits by his costume designer of many years, Bill Belew. (Below) Elvis greets fans in Hawaii before his Aloha From Hawaii concert. (Opposite page) Elvis pals around with Muhammad Ali in Vegas.

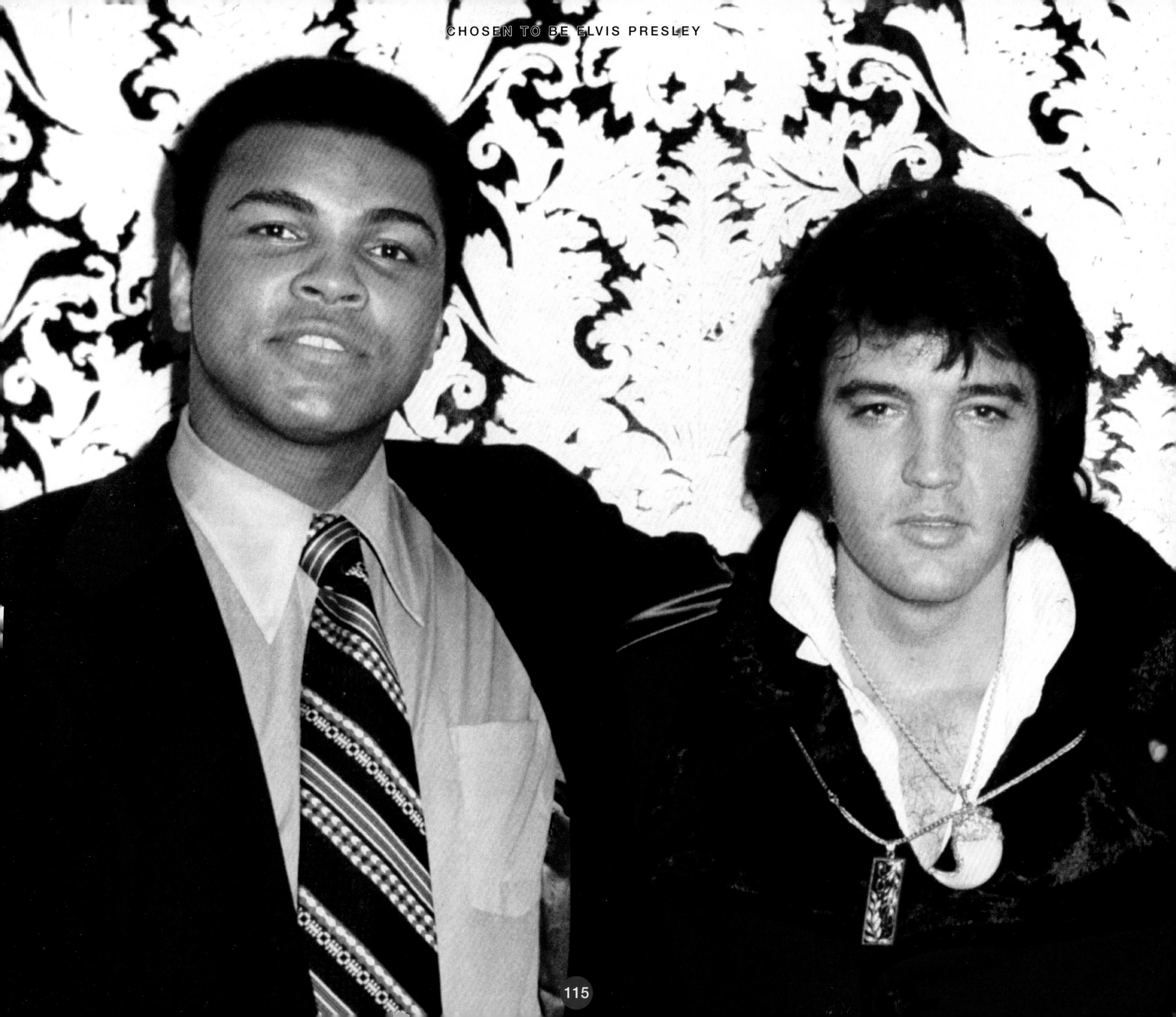

ALOHA FROM HAWAII

The anticipation for the show was growing by the day. The Colonel wanted a circus-type atmosphere around the whole thing, and he would get it. "The vibes in the air were just immeasurable," said NBC director Marty Pasetta in *Careless Love*.

Elvis continued to be caught up in the excitement as well, and arrived in the islands five days before the show was to be aired. He looked fit and ready, having lost 25 pounds since his Vegas gig ended. There would be two shows, actually, one of which would serve as a backup in case anything went wrong with the feed on the second. And, there was no admission charge. Fans were only to make a contribution to the Kui Lee Cancer Fund, in honor of a Hawaiian composer who died of the disease while still in his 30s. A total of $75,000 would be raised for the fund.

(Left) Elvis liked Hawaii and Hawaii liked Elvis; between filming for movies, charity concerts and his Aloha special, Elvis spent a good deal of time in paradise. (Below) Elvis wore his "American Eagle" jumpsuit for the Aloha concert.

PURE GOLD

ELVIS

2 RECORD SET

ELVIS IN CONC

ORIGINAL SOUNDTRACK RECORDING
CBS-TV SPECIAL PLUS ADDITION
RECORDED ON TOUR JUN

THE NATIONAL ACADEMY
OF
RDING ARTS   CES

presents this certificate to

ELVIS PRESLEY

in recognition of

NOMINATION

for the

BEST VOCAL PERFORMANCE
GLE RECORD OR TRACK - MALE

ARE YOU LONESOME TONIGHT?

for the awards period

1960

THE NATIONAL ACADEMY
OF
RECORDING ARTS AND SCIENCES

presents this certificate to

ELVIS PRESLEY

in recognition of

NOMINATION

for the

BEST PERFORM
Y A POP SING

ARE YOU LONESO

196

THE NATIONAL ACADEMY
OF
RECORDING ARTS AND SCIENCES

The first show, taped in front of a live audience, was impressive, but it was nothing like the second, which would be live.

It started at 12:30 a.m., which was probably all right for Elvis since he was a notorious night owl in the first place. The starting time was to accommodate live audiences in the Far East. The rest of the world — the United States and Europe — would get a slightly expanded version on delay.

Elvis, in his action-hero costume topped by his black helmet of hair, perhaps didn't give his most spirited performance, but the audience didn't seem to mind. It was "long on music, loud on screams," reported the *Honolulu Advertiser*. The highlight came when he tossed his $10,000 cape into the crowd where it was caught by, of all people, a sportswriter from the *Advertiser*.

The numbers for the show were absolutely staggering. In the United States, the show drew 57 percent of the viewing audience — more than watched the moon landing in 1969 — and the ratings were similar in 30 European countries. The ratings in the Far East, however, were even more startling: 91.8 percent in the Philippines, 70 percent in Hong Kong, 70 to 80 percent in Korea. The estimated number who watched came in as predicted, 1.5 billion.

(Preceding page) Elvis' three Grammy Awards, on display at Graceland, were all for gospel music, which is surprising considering his impact on the pop and rock charts. (Below) Elvis had grown up with gospel, and sang it at most of his shows.

popularity, despite his longevity, despite his No. 1 songs and No. 1 albums, he had won only three Grammys in his career, and all of them were for gospel songs.

Elvis began his final tour in the summer of 1977, and the final stop was in Indianapolis on June 26. Afterward, he complained of being tired and not feeling well, and he returned to Graceland.

It was there, in his beloved home, that he died on August 16, 1977. He was only 42 years old.

(Left) Elvis was a deeply religious and spiritual person; gospel music, the music he had sung his whole life, often moved him. (Opposite page) Elvis left this world too soon, but his passion for music and performance can be seen to this day in his songs and movies, and he continues to add to his legions of fans.

"HOW GREAT THOU ART"

On Oct. 9 that same year, their divorce became final. Six days later, he was hospitalized for pneumonia, pleurisy, an enlarged colon and hepatitis. It was the start of many health problems he would have over the next few years as he continued to play Las Vegas and tour. Elvis battled both weight and health problems, including an increasing dependency upon prescription drugs, according to Elvis.com.

He kept going, though, and in 1974, he received his third Grammy Award, this time for the live version of "How Great Thou Art" on "Recorded Live on Stage in Memphis." Despite his enormous

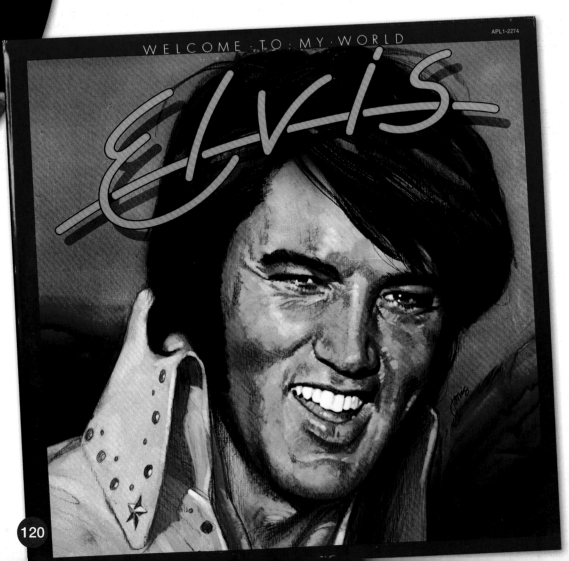

A Genuine Cultural Force

At Elvis' funeral Aug. 18, estimates of mourners lining the Memphis streets and gathered outside Graceland ranged as high as 80,000. People climbed trees to get a better view as the bronze casket was wheeled into the mansion. The mourning was worldwide, and this was before the 24-hour cable news cycle and the Internet. There was really nothing to compare it to at the time.

The local telephone company asked that people restrict their phone calls because of the stress on the incoming lines. Florists had more requests for flowers than they could handle. The local limousine services had to go out of town to get more white cars — there were only three in the city and 17 were needed. Elvis' father, Vernon, had insisted everything be in white, from the funeral procession down to his burial suit.

After a private viewing by the family and close associates, the public was allowed to view the body four at time. National Guardsmen helped to guide the mourners, and a sea of flowers covered the front lawn.

Thousands filed through for the viewing, which was supposed to end at 4:30 in the afternoon, but the time was extended to 6 p.m. Not every fan gathered could be admitted, but people seemed to respect the sanctity of the moment when the police finally closed the gates. The official funeral was scheduled for the next day, a private service attended by 200 or so.

Elvis was buried in Forest Hill Cemetery in a mausoleum near his mother, Gladys. But a few days later their remains were moved Graceland's Memorial Garden where they remain today.

For anyone less than a head of state, it was an unprecedented outpouring. Graceland remains a huge draw every Jan. 8 — his birthday — and Aug. 16 — the date of his death. To some, a visit to Graceland is akin to a pilgrimage to the Mecca of rock 'n' roll. Many of his fans — and many more who weren't even born in 1977 — are now older but still have that Elvis twinkle in their eyes. More than 600,000 a year come through gates of the mansion, now an attraction dedicated to the King of Rock 'n' Roll.

What remains, then, is an argument that has raged since cavemen began blowing through animal horns and beating on skin drums: Who had the most influence on popular music? Mozart or Beethoven? Benny Goodman or Glenn Miller? Frank Sinatra or Bing Crosby?

Put aside the others and just consider the legacy of Elvis.

Rock and roll was already making its way into the national consciousness before he made his big splash in 1956. It's just that he turned the new music into a phenomenon — and he made it arrive faster and bigger.

He came on the scene with a totally new style, and no one at first seemed to know what to make of it. Here was a gyrating kid from the South singing something dubbed rockabilly, and crowds all over the land were responding like few other audiences had ever done over a performer.

He was selling records, a lot of records, even to kids who had nothing on which to play them. *Uncut* magazine in 2005 rated the first performance of "Heartbreak Hotel" as the No. 2 cultural event of the rock 'n' roll era. His appearances on television shows drew record audiences. He sold millions of single records and millions more of albums — more than a billion total, according to *Billboard.* His "Aloha from Hawaii" concert brought in 1.5 billion viewers worldwide.

Elvis was the first megastar on the rock scene, and the ones who followed looked up to him. Many of the very biggest names in the industry acknowledged as much.

"Nothing really affected me until I heard Elvis," John Lennon once said. "If there hadn't been an Elvis, there wouldn't have been a Beatles."

Rod Stewart: "Elvis was the King. No doubt about it. People like myself, Mick Jagger and all the others only followed in his footsteps."

Said Bob Dylan: "Hearing him for the first time was like busting out of jail."

The famed composer Leonard Bernstein once told an interviewer, "Elvis is the greatest cultural force in the twentieth century."

"Elvis is the greatest cultural force in the twentieth century."

— *Composer Leonard Bernstein*

All of these accolades were directed toward someone who played the guitar and piano by ear and couldn't read music. But he was possessed with an uncanny ear, a distinctive voice and an unerring sense of the musical histories that motivated him, like the blues and gospel songs of which he was so fond.

The main thing was his voice. "He could imitate anything he heard. He had a perfect ear," said songwriter Jerry Leiber, who co-wrote many Elvis songs.

"He could sing anything," gospel singer Shawn Neilson told another interviewer. "I've never seen such versatility. ... He had the ability to make everyone in the audience think that he was singing directly to them."

There was also a distinct non-musical cultural contribution Elvis made to society — helping in his way, the civil rights movement.

Some have claimed that he "stole" black music from those who were toiling in the shadows. Many of the major black entertainers of the time, however, would disagree.

Little Richard was one. He had every right to claim his music had been stolen, primarily by Pat Boone, while he had been effectively banned from the white airwaves. To Little Richard, Elvis "was an integrator, Elvis was a blessing. They wouldn't let black music through. He opened the door for black music."

Al Green agreed. "He broke the ice for all of us."

It wasn't long before Little Richard, Green and Fats Domino were fixtures on the airwaves with their own songs. In fact, after Elvis made his triumphant return to the stage in Las Vegas in 1969, he was referred to as the "King" in an after-concert press conference. "No," said Elvis, "I'm not. The real King is right there," pointing to a beaming Fats Domino standing in the background.

Today, more than three decades after his death, the fans still come. Some still can't believe Elvis is gone. Early on there was a rash of Elvis sightings around the world.

His death also spawned a whole new form of entertainment — Elvis tribute artists, the best of which compete each year in The Ultimate Elvis Tribute Artist Contest during Elvis Week.

One of the more unique tribute-artists groups is "The Flying Elvi," a 10-member team of skydivers who will leap into just about any gathering and who give new meaning to the word "jumpsuit."

In the end, though, the real legacy of Elvis is his music.

More than 35 years after his death people young and old still recognize it, still sing it, still buy it. In 1994, the 40th anniversary of "That's All Right," the record was re-released and sailed into the top 10 best-sellers. As recently as 2005, three of his songs — "Jailhouse Rock," "One Night/I Got Stung," and "It's Now or Never" — all made No. 1 in re-release in the U.K.

"Elvis 30 #1 Hits," originally released in 2002, has sold 10 million copies, and "Elvis Second to None," which was released in 2003, has sold 4 million. Both continue to be strong sellers. In September 2007, "Elvis: the King" was released internationally only and appeared on the top 10 album charts in 12 countries. He has even gone online. In 2007 Celine Dion performed a duet of "If I Can Dream" with a taped Elvis on "American Idol." It became the most downloaded video on iTunes for two weeks, and nearly 10 million unique visitors go to Elvis.com each year.

He remains the best-selling deceased celebrity in the world, which may seem a dubious distinction, but which is further proof his memory is still very much alive.

On the 25th anniversary of his death in 2002, the *New York Times* — at one time among his harshest critics — wrote an editorial which put Elvis in perspective:

"To those too young to have experienced Elvis Presley in his prime, today's celebration of his death must seem peculiar. ... [He was] a genuine cultural force. ... Elvis's breakthroughs are underappreciated because in this rock-and-roll age, his hard-rocking music and sultry style have triumphed so completely."

A silver Cadillac led the funeral cortege through Memphis and down Elvis Presley Boulevard on Aug. 18, 1977. The hearse was white as were the 17 limousines that followed.
Elvis had insisted that everything at his funeral be in white. It was estimated 80,000 people lined the route and surrounded Graceland that day. (Inset) Priscilla and Lisa Marie arrive for the funeral.

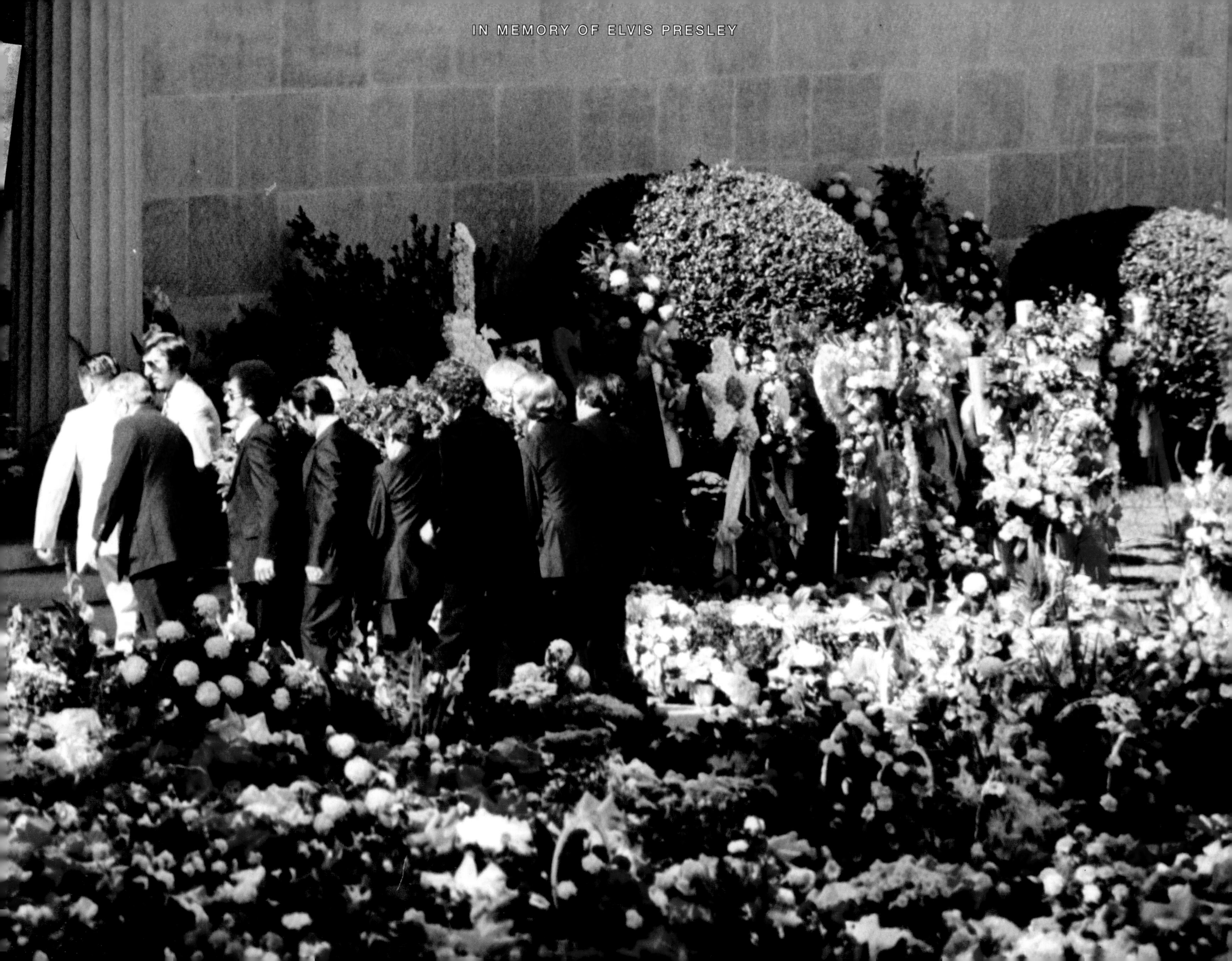

IN MEMORY OF ELVIS PRESLEY

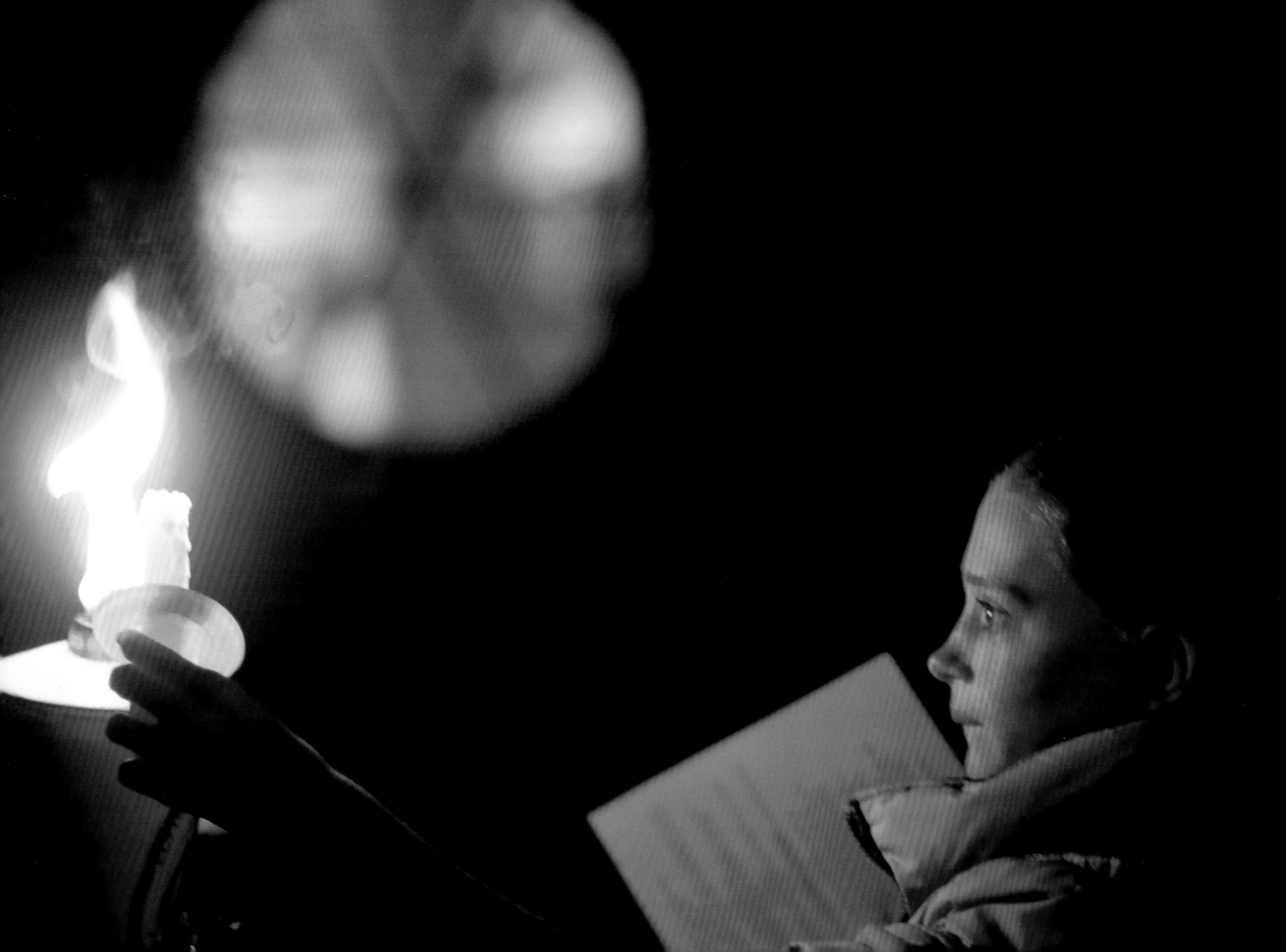

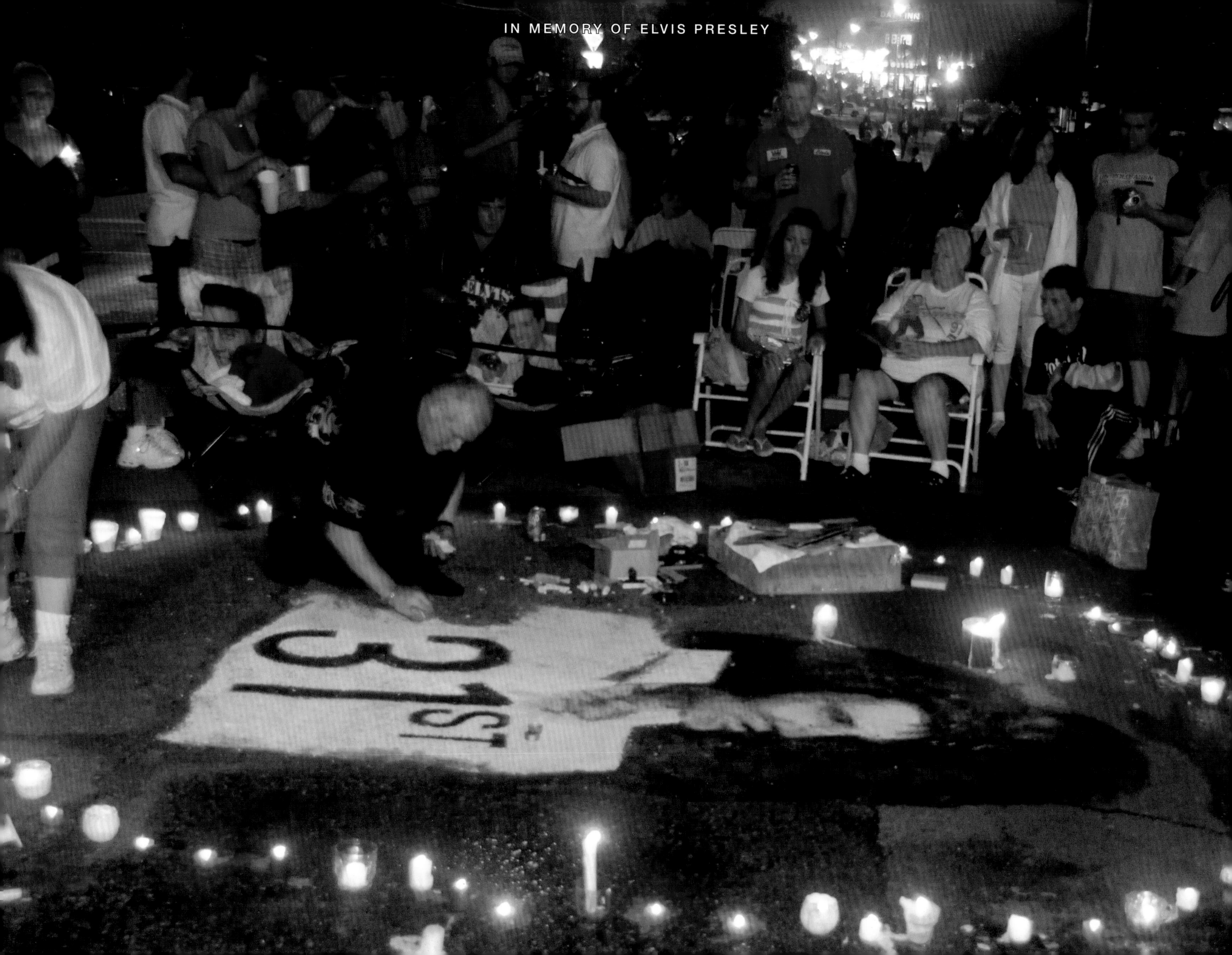
31ST

Flowers and memorials mount every August at the grave of Elvis in the Memorial Garden at Graceland. To the right of his grave is that of his father, Vernon, who died in 1979.
To the left lay his grandmother, Minnie Mae, who died in 1980. Elvis' mother, Gladys, is also buried in the garden.

Elvis bought Graceland in 1957 for a reported $103,500. The mansion stands on 13.8 acres of land in the Whitehaven community of Memphis. The house has even been celebrated in song, most notably by Paul Simon in his album "Graceland." The title song depicts it as a holy place and won a Grammy for Simon in 1987.

Priscilla Presley addresses the crowd during the ceremonies when Graceland was officially turned into a museum. The house originally had 23 rooms with eight bedrooms and eight baths, but Elvis made extensive additions and renovations once he moved there in '57. Graceland was named a National Historic Landmark in 2006.

Dozens of Elvis' gold records and albums line the walls in Graceland. The Hall of Gold where the records are displayed was formerly the racquetball court, which Elvis had built after he moved there in 1957. Elvis expanded the original Graceland from just more than 10,000-square feet to more than 17,500-square feet.

Double Trouble, MGM 1967

Taking advantage of the latest craze for discotheque dancing and spy movies during the mid-1960s, the producers of *Double Trouble* combined the two fads to form the basic plot of this musical. Elvis plays Guy Lambert, a pop singer who becomes involved with intrigue while playing the discotheque scene in London and Antwerp. Guy's problems begin when he meets heiress Jill Conway, played by young Annette Day, who has a crush on the singer much to the chagrin of her guardian. Jill leads Guy through numerous adventures involving spies, counterspies, jewel thieves and harebrained detectives. The latter, played by the zany Wiere Brothers, provide the film's comic relief. Eventually, Jill succeeds in casting her spell over Guy and the two marry. Based on a novel by Mark Brandel, the working title was *You're Killing Me* and the idea was to give the movie the same feel as that of the zany comedic Beatles films *Hard Days Night* and *Help*.

One of the youngest actresses to ever costar with Elvis, Annette Day was just 18 years old when she acted in *Double Trouble*. Her only prior acting experience had consisted of doing the Charleston in a Christmas concert at school. Elvis did take an interest in Day during filming, though not in the romantic sense. He surprised her near the end of shooting with a white Mustang as a remembrance of her first film experience.

No Presley museum would be complete without a collection of memories from his movies from the 1950s and '60s. He starred in 31 of them from 1956, "Love Me Tender," to 1969, "Change of Habit." The photo on the left shows Elvis with Annette Day in 1967's "Double Trouble." It was the only movie Day ever appeared in.

The band and singers jam along with a tape of Elvis from his historic "Aloha from Hawaii" concert in 1973.
That concert was one of the most successful ever, seen by an estimated 1.5 billion people worldwide.

Mrs. Tennessee 2008, Cydney Miller, celebrates Elvis Week with a quartet of young fans.
The annual festival has become popular with families from across the country.

Part of most week's activities is a screening on the green. Here, the audience takes in one of Elvis' earliest films, "Jailhouse Rock." His co-star was Judy Tyler, shown on the screen with Elvis. She was killed in an automobile accident a few weeks after the shooting wrapped, an event that so upset Elvis, he refused to watch the completed version of the film.

ELVIS WAS IN THE BUILDING

It was in the early spring of 1956 when KLTF — 960 on your dial — in Little Falls, Minnesota, decided to try some new programming on Saturday afternoon, something the station could plug in after the final pig market reports, which were important news — "Welcome to Little Falls! The Biggest Little Pig Market in the World!" proclaimed the billboard on the outskirts of town.

The station decided to try a one-hour show called "The Teen Top Ten" to be hosted — gratis — by a local teenager, me. They were well aware of this growing phenomenon on the musical and cultural landscape called "rock 'n' roll." Kids all over town and around the county were straining their car radios at night to pick up a station from the Twin Cities broadcasting the new music, and KLTF wanted to get a least a small slice of that pie.

Rock 'n' roll wasn't that old, but it wasn't brand new, either. Bill Haley and the Comets had a monster hit with "Rock Around the Clock" in 1955, and Pat Boone, that All-American boy in white bucks, had begun to cover Little Richard and Fats Domino songs.

Anyway, the station put out ballot boxes all around the county and the kids voted for their favorites. I would count the ballots, and the results would be the Teen Top Ten for the week. The kids took to the idea — you could at least pick up KLTF in the daytime — and in March the first show hit the air featuring "Why Do Fools Fall in Love?" by Frankie Lymon and the Teenagers at No. 1.

It was the next week when it began. This new guy, Elvis Presley, hit No. 1 with "Heartbreak Hotel." It would be two years or so before any other artist — this was voting by kids in the farm country of Minnesota, not *Billboard* — took over the top spot. No one had ever seen anything like it, and I still haven't.

Whenever Elvis was scheduled to be on a television show — Stage Show, Steve Allen, Ed Sullivan — you did not want to be on the sidewalk around 6, lest you be trampled by a bevy of teenage girls in their poodle skirts beating a path to a friend's house, one that had a TV set.

The phenomenon just kept escalating. The girls bought Elvis' records, even though they didn't have record players. Eventually they would buy those little, square players on which to spin their 45s.

Things reached a crescendo in 1956 when the first Elvis movie, "Love Me Tender," came out. It took a while to get to Little Falls (it didn't make it until early '57), but when it did, you couldn't get in the theater for all of the screaming bobby-soxers. You certainly couldn't hear a word of the movie if you did.

Elvis was in the building, and for some, he never left.

—*Frank Hyland*
LFHS, Class of '58

LITTLE FALLS, MINNESOTA

260

About The Author

Frank Hyland is a veteran of more than 40 years in the newspaper wars, and one who thankfully retired before the newspapers lost the battle. He is a native Minnesotan who grew up in the farm town of Little Falls in the central part of the state. After college and a stint in the U.S. Army stationed in Berlin as a Russian interpreter, Hyland came back to Little Falls and, failing to find any gainful employment there as an interpreter, entered the news business as the sports editor of the *Little Falls Daily Transcript*. From there, it was on to St. Cloud, Minnesota, and West Palm Beach, Florida, where it was far warmer and far more boring. Then came an offer from the *Atlanta Journal*, where he would stay for the next 35 years until it folded. During that time, he worked mostly as a sportswriter covering the pros — basketball (the Atlanta Hawks), football (the Falcons), baseball (the Braves) and samplings of other pro sports, including soccer, hockey, NASCAR and the PGA and LPGA tours, not to mention a tractor pull or two. In 1991, during the first Gulf War, he was temporarily assigned to the *Journal* news desk where he would stay — temporarily — for the next 12 years editing and writing for the news side. When the paper folded, so did Hyland, retiring in 2003. Hyland is also the author of a biography of another Southern icon, humorist Lewis Grizzard — an old friend with whom he worked for many years — entitled *The Sportin' Life of Lewis Grizzard*. Hyland lives in Buckhead with his lovely wife Maxine and his lovable mutt border collie Uschi. He has two grown daughters, Tracy Lojek and Shannon Hyland, and two grandchildren, John and Addison.

Acknowledgments

This was a project — no matter the popularity and familiarity of Elvis Presley — that anyone doing such a book needs a lot of help, and a lot of people gave me that help.

Thanks to the people at Elvis Presley Enterprises who so lovingly treasure the King and who were kind enough to check for any inaccuracies that may have been in the manuscript.

Thanks, too, to Mary Warner of the Morrison Country Historical Society in Minnesota who took the time to locate the old photos from my old stomping ground.

I owe a special debt to a man whom I have never met, but would like to, Peter Guralnick, the author of the two-part Elvis biography, *Last Train to Memphis* and *Careless Love*. If you are a fan of Elvis, get both volumes. They are truly special and extremely well written, something I guess I could be a bit jealous of.

Of course, there is my wife, Maxine, who kept me going and gave me that occasional kick in the backside that I need.

And finally, my dog Uschi, who slept behind my desk chair the whole time instead of insisting on going out every five minutes only to come right back in five seconds later as she usually does. It helped the concentration.

— *Frank Hyland*

Bibliography

· Alagna, Magdalena. *Elvis Presley*. Rosen Publishing Group, 2002.
· Bertrand, Michael T. *Race, Rock, and Elvis*. University of Illinois Press, 2000.
· Cook, J., Henry, P. *Graceland National Historic Landmark Nomination Form*, 2004.
· *Elvis: Commemorative Edition*. Publications International, 2001.
· Guralnick, Peter. *Last Train to Memphis: The Rise of Elvis Presley*. Boston: Little, Brown and Company, 1994.
· Guralnick, Peter. *Careless Love. The Unmaking of Elvis Presley*. Back Bay Books, 1999.
· Guralnick, Peter, and Jorengsen, Ernst. *Elvis Day-By-Day: The Definitive Record of His Life and Music*. The Ballantine Publishing Group, 1999.
· Jorgensen, Ernst. *Elvis Presley: A life in music. The complete recording sessions*. St. Martin's Press, 1998.
· Matthew-Walker, Robert. *Elvis Presley. A Study in Music*. Tunbridge Wells: Midas Books, 1979.
· Presley, Priscilla. *Elvis and Me*. New York: G.P. Putnam's Sons, 1985.
· Elvis.com. *http://www.elvis.com*. (Accessed summer 2009).